TWIN CITY

A PICTORIAL HISTORY OF EAST CHICAGO, INDIANA

In 1907, four out of every five residents of the Twin City were born in foreign countries, as the municipality of East Chicago, Indiana, became the quintessential American melting pot. Naturally, Old Country culture was immediately transplanted into Twin City soil, and quickly became visible in churches, clubs, neighborhoods, and celebrations. This culture, slightly Americanized, was continued by the American-born children of the immigrants, who, by 1930, outnumbered foreign-born residents about three to two; together, foreign-born and the children of foreign-born then constituted three out of five Twin City residents. Today, slightly more than a century after East Chicago came into existence as a village, Old Country culture is still deeply rooted in Twin City society, as new immigrants and the Americanized children and grandchildren and great-grandchildren of earlier immigrants perpetuate the customs, manners, ideals, skills, and arts of faraway places. The young women here, all employees of Inland Steel, are shown during Christmas 1952 in the costumes of the lands of their ancestors. Clockwise: Czechoslovakia, Lithuania, Norway, Hungary, Poland, Greece, Italy, Yugoslavia, and Mexico. Photo from Inland Steel Company

TWIN CITY

A PICTORIAL HISTORY OF EAST CHICAGO, INDIANA

By Archibald McKinlay

THE
DONNING COMPANY
PUBLISHERS
NORFOLK/VIRGINIA BEACH

The Donning Company/Publishers
5659 Virginia Beach Boulevard
Norfolk, Virginia, 23502

Edited by Tony Lillis
Richard A. Horwege, Senior Editor

Library of Congress Cataloging-in-Publication Data

McKinlay, Archibald.
    Twin City: a pictorial history of East Chicago, Indiana/
    by Archibald McKinlay; [edited by Tony Lillis].
    p.   cm.
    Bibliography: p.
    Includes index.
    ISBN 0-89865-583-8 (lim. ed.)
    1. East Chicago (Ind.)—History—Pictorial works. 2. East Chicago
(Ind.)—Description—Views. I. Lillis, Tony. II. Title.
F534.E15M35   1988   87-36586
977.2′99—dc 19   CIP

Printed in the United States of America

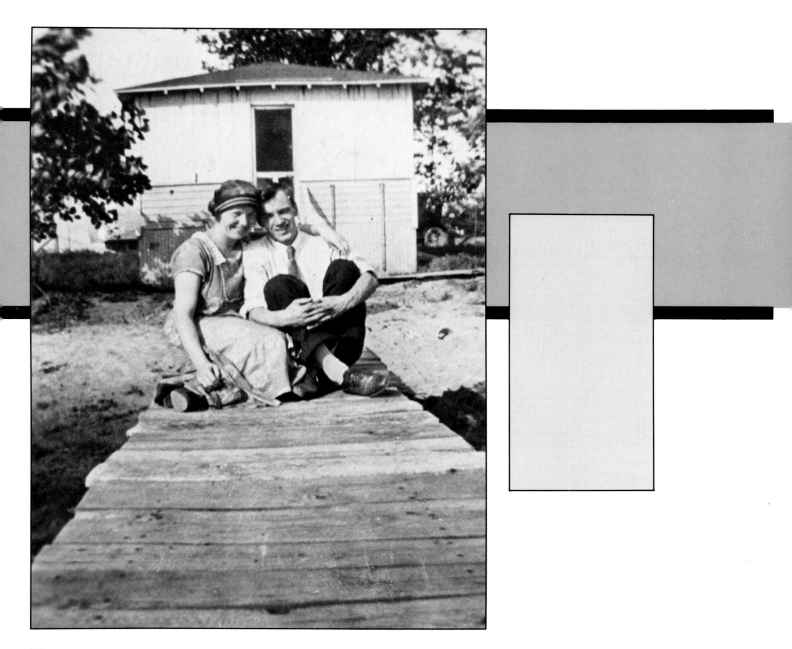

To
Margaret Stewart (McLean) McKinlay
and Archibald McKinlay, III, my parents,
who came to the Twin City
from Scotland as young adults
and enriched it every day
of their lives.

Shortly after the turn of the century, all land companies associated with the creation of the Twin City were merged into the East Chicago Company. The first company (1881) was the East Chicago Improvement Company, a bit of deliberately confusing nomenclature designed to tap into the positive values associated with rapidly selling Chicago real estate, but which subsequently often caused confusion without the positive values. That first company began, in 1887, the Calumet Canal and Improvement Company and also the Standard Steel and Iron Company. In the mid-1890s, the Lake Michigan Land Company came into existence. When all of these companies were merged, they took on a name that sounded remarkably like the original company, and conducted business out of offices in the Tod Opera House in East Chicago and the building shown here at the corner of Michigan and Pennsylvania avenues in Indiana Harbor. Photo by Buchstaber from the East Chicago Historical Society

CONTENTS

ACKNOWLEDGMENTS

Robert A. Pastrick, Mayor
City of East Chicago

What you are reading is the first and only history (or approximation of it) of one of the most remarkable cities of this or any other time, East Chicago, Indiana, the Twin City. Over a century of hyperactivity, people who lived and worked in the Twin City seem to have been too busy living the present to record it, much less think of the present as history in the making. Fortunately, they took photographs. And a few kept scrapbooks. And a select extremely long-lived few could call on information etched on long, retentive memories, recollections that are not only accurate but verifiable.

Thus, the information in this volume is the distillation of many ransacked attics and basements and garages, more than a hundred taped interviews, and endless hours at the microfilm machine, as well as the usual rummaging through of old books, pamphlets, and periodicals. The mother lode, though, was the East Chicago Historical Society, which may be the most under-appreciated, most productive resource of not only Twin City history but history of the many lands who sent their young and strong and often best to the Twin City. Through many years of volunteer work by Ezelyn Johnston and Gertrude Weber, supported by sometimes-historian, sometimes-president, Rose Levan, the files (including audiotapes and photographs) are precisely organized and indexed, a blessing of no small consequence to a rummager. Lately, Charles L. Dahlin, the Society's president, has encouraged this magnificent resource, and Theodore Mason, head librarian of the East Chicago library system, was instrumental in finding the Society's collections a home in a new addition to the main library, called the Indiana Room.

For photographs, I especially thank Merry Barickman, who solicited and coordinated candidate photos for the book, and generally served as photo editor and copy reviewer. I also thank Armando Lopez, who took time out from his flourishing career as a free-lance photographer to relentlessly copy and print hundreds of candidate photos. I thank, too, Dee Shepherd, who helped in the preliminary planning of the book and screening of photographs, and Irv Lewin, who kindly used his popular radio program on station W.J.O.B. to solicit photos.

I especially thank Austin Boyle, who provided all of the information for the post World War II period, screened all of the photographs, and reviewed all of the final copy. Until other commitments preempted his time, Austin was to have been co-author of this book.

Finally, I thank as profusely as I can Patricia McKinlay, my wife and live-in grant, who edited all of the copy, edited the photos and captions, and generally subsidized the creation of the book.

Others who contributed photos are credited throughout the book.

Archibald McKinlay
Chicago, Illinois

Robert A. Pastrick

MAYOR

4527 INDIANAPOLIS BLVD.
EAST CHICAGO, INDIANA 46312

Our founders designed the Twin City of East Chicago and Indiana Harbor to be the perfect industrial community, and it has been. It became one of the finest expressions of an Industrial Age that began after the Civil War and is only now ending. As one economic development expert recently said, if the ideal industrial park were to be designed, it would be precisely what already exists in the Twin City. But times change, and the Twin City is changing, too. In the 1980s, the Twin City has been making the transition from the Industrial Age to the Information Age. And it is doing so with all the vigor of its rich and vigorous past.

What you will find in this pictorial history is prologue. It is the beginning of our future. You will gain from it some sense of the ultimate American melting pot, where a hundred nationalities and races combined to make the Twin City the very essence of what America is all about. You will find opportunity in abundance, production beyond comparison, a few disappointments and failures, and an eternal striving for improvement. Above all, you will find change and a municipality that not only adapts to change but one that has made adaptation a way of life.

East Chicago, Indiana began as a settlement in 1888, as a town in 1889, and as a city in 1893. The book you have in your hands is an indispensible reference in celebrating the centennials of these three events. It is a story about a dream come true, and a promise of rebirth.

Robert A. Pastrick, Mayor
City of East Chicago

1

UNIDENTICAL TWINS

An industrial canal physically divides the Twin City, the main leg running from Lake Michigan (top of photo) southwesterly to a fork, where one branch runs due south to the Grand Calumet River and another runs due west toward Lake George. Territory west of the south leg is called East Chicago; territory east of the main leg and south leg is called Indiana Harbor. Photo from the Stuart Thomson Studios

The first babies born in East Chicago were twins, William Torrence O'Brien and Redmond Walsh O'Brien. It was an omen. Their birth augured a dual community unlike any in the United States, two cities within one municipality. East Chicago is thus called the Twin City.

The twins are fraternal, however, not identical. They developed from separately-fertilized socio-economic ova, and so display distinctive hereditary characteristics. Nor were the twins born at the same time. The older twin came into being in the late nineteenth century, the younger thirteen years later in the early twentieth. Moreover, although they share a common government, the twins developed physically and psychologically apart, separated by a ship canal, a lack of easy communication, and different blood lines.

To further complicate the bringing forth of this different kind of municipality, East Chicago is both the whole and a part. The name "East Chicago" designates the municipality, but it also designates the elder twin and the west side of the municipality. Indiana Harbor, the younger twin, is the east side of the municipality and illogically the larger twin.

For most of its history, the municipality of East Chicago has grown by twos. What existed in one twin existed in the other, usually in a variant form. Commercially, each twin had its own, discrete downtown, the center of each confusingly called by the same name: The Four Corners. Industrially, pioneer East Chicago factories huddled compactly together in a neat plot that became the core of the community. Indiana Harbor factories, on the other hand, surround a core of residences; the Harbor factories, which were generally much larger than East Chicago factories, sprawled out and stretched into all corners of the community, and even all the way across the city line into Buffington, technically part of Gary but economically and spiritually part of Indiana Harbor.

Government services also arrived in pairs. Shortly after East Chicago attained city status in 1893, the city council formalized a volunteer fire department and provided volunteers with hand-drawn hose carts and hand pumps, housed in different parts of the community. A coded whistle atop Penman's Tank Works directed the firefighters to the fire. After running for their equipment, the volunteers then pushed the equipment-filled carts to the scene of the fire, typically in the nick of time. Their overall success was enhanced by not having to worry about fire hydrants. Since early East Chicago was three-fourths water, the volunteers simply stuck their hoses into nearby sloughs and pumped away.

Indiana Harbor's fire department followed a similar course of development, but with less success. Unlike the decentralized equipment system of East Chicago, Indiana Harbor's was centralized at Maxwell's Livery Stables. When the whistle atop the water works sounded, the Indiana Harbor laddies ran for Maxwell's, pushed the equipment through the slow sand, and usually arrived at the scene of the fire in time to watch the building metamorphose into throbbing embers.

Although politically one body, each twin not only had its own police department and lock-up, but its own post office. A person sending mail to the west side of the municipality addressed it to East Chicago, and a person sending mail to the east side addressed it to Indiana Harbor. The logic of this had to do with time. Since they were located on all the trunk lines from the East, Indiana Harbor industries could receive mail much faster than had their missives gone nonstop to Chicago, then back to East Chicago, and then over uncertain terrain to Indiana

Harbor. Of course, each twin also had its own railroad stations; the Pennsylvania Railroad even had stations in both East Chicago and Indiana Harbor.

For recreation, the twins had their own swimming holes. For a long time though, Indiana Harbor had the best of it. Situated right on Lake Michigan, the Harbor boasted a sand and rock beach that was part of fifteen hundred feet of lake frontage. (The east end of the frontage was called B.A.B., and used for skinny dipping.) Because the canal and railroad freight yards blocked East Chicagoans from easy access to the beach, the Board of Park Commissioners finally (in 1924-1925) built East Chicago a fancy swimming hole of its own, a 150 by 50 foot, recyling swimming pool in Tod Park, with an attached forty-two by forty-six foot bathhouse. They placed the pool in an area that also featured lagoons and a nine-hole golf course, and they ran the pool free of charge.

With the swimming advantage now having gone to East Chicago, it was only a matter of time until Indiana Harbor had a pool too, and in 1939 a more elaborate pool than the one in Tod Park appeared in the Harbor's Washington Park. This led to building a similar pool in East Chicago's Kosiusko Park, followed by still another in Indiana Harbor's George Washington Carver Park of the New Addition. Had it not been for the intervention of World War II, with the halting of all such projects, the municipality might have become as liquid as when its developers first went to work on it.

A swimming hole, incidentally, determined the location of the City Hall, one of the Twin City's few one-of-a-kind facilities. When leaders of the municipality finally decided that a proper place to conduct municipal affairs should be built, both twins insisted that it arise in their respective territories. The argument raged loud and long, with more-populous Indiana Harbor seeming to have gained the advantage. The Harborites traded that advantage, however, for the development of a lakefront park to go with their beach. Thus, the Harbor got Lees Park, and East Chicago got City Hall. It was built in 1908 and, of course, East Chicago called it the finest in the state.

In a more cultural vein, each twin had a women's club, dedicated to the local promotion of music, literature, home economics, and civics. In East Chicago, the Tuesday Reading Club (1905) merged in 1912 with the Music Club (1911) to form the East Chicago Woman's Club. In Indiana Harbor, the Woman's Club (1908) merged in 1913 with the Round Table Club (1911) to form the Indiana Harbor Woman's Club. Both clubs dedicated themselves to gaining libraries for their respective territories. They both succeeded, two libraries being established March 1, 1909, one in the new City Hall in East Chicago, the other over a new fire station in Indiana Harbor. And when Andrew Carnegie donated forty thousand dollars for a library, the gift was naturally divided, with a pair of similar-looking buildings being erected, one on the Circle at Chicago and Baring avenues in East Chicago, the other on the corner of Grapevine (Grand Boulevard) and 136th Street in the Harbor. Both libraries began with an essentially equal number of books, the East Chicago library with 3,967 volumes, the Harbor library with 3,456 volumes. Both buildings had tile roofs and were made of red vitrified brick. Both were dedicated in 1913 on successive days, the East Chicago library on May 16, the Indiana Harbor building the following evening.

Churches also sprang up in pairs. The first church in East Chicago was the Methodist Episcopal Church (1889), with services first held in the Tod Opera House. When the first church was organized in Indiana Harbor (1902), it too was a Methodist Episcopal church. The first Roman Catholic church in East Chicago, St Mary's (1888), had an Irish congregation; the first Catholic church in Indiana Harbor, St. Patrick's (1902), also had an Irish congregation. The first Catholic church in East Chicago whose congregation spoke a foreign language was St. Michaels (1896), which was quickly renamed St. Stanislaus, and its members were Polish; the first non-English speaking Catholic church in Indiana Harbor was St. John Cantius (1903), and it likewise was Polish.

Although it took awhile, the high schools came as a pair, Washington in Indiana Harbor and Roosevelt in East Chicago. Before Indiana Harbor existed, a high school was organized in East Chicago and classes held in the Tod Opera House. Then the North Side School, later called the Benjamin Harrison School, was built and opened just a month after the turn of the century, in February, 1900. After the advent of Indiana Harbor in 1901, pupils from the Harbor traveled circuitously to East Chicago in a rickety trolley car to attend East Chicago High School in the Harrison building. Thirteen years later, well after the Harbor's population overtook that of East Chicago, East Chicago High School met in the Washington School building (1908), and the commuting process was reversed, with East Chicago pupils shake-rattling-and-rolling their way by trolley to the Harbor.

Washington expanded prodigiously when the east half of a new high school was built in 1918, a west half and a shop in 1920, and an auditorium and gym in 1924. Additionally, the first year of college was offered in the new complex. (A technical building was added in 1939.) By 1925, however, the municipality achieved academic parity when Roosevelt High School was built in East Chicago, contiguous to Tod Park, which gave Roosevelt a campus more idyllic than most colleges. Indeed, Roosevelt housed in 1932 an extension of Indiana University, and a separate I.U. building was erected in Tod Park in 1939-1940.

For more than sixty years the rivalry between Washington and Roosevelt in debating, music, theater, scholarship, and sports was gloriously intense. The Brown Derby, a trophy that passed to the winner of the Roosevelt-Washington football game each year, was coveted by some partisans more ardently than a conference championship.

The sibling twins never stopped competing with each other, and the competition extended well beyond the schools. It was most apparent in competition for business, evidenced by the extraordinary fact that the Twin City had two different chambers of commerce. Interestingly, the first chamber came into existence in the younger twin. Organized originally as the Booster Club, it became in 1908 the Commercial Club of Indiana Harbor and East Chicago and met at its own handsome and commodious clubhouse on Guthrie Street. Within a year, however, East Chicago spun off its own chamber, at first called the East Chicago Business Men's Association, organized February 12, 1909. It would not be until after World War I that the two clubs merged into the East Chicago Chamber of Commerce, which was for more than half a century, according to its partisans, the strongest chamber in Indiana.

Of all the differences in the fraternal twins of East Chicago and Indiana Harbor, however, the most fundamental was the way the bloods of different races and nationalities mingled within each twin. Both twins had predominently foreign-born populations, but one twin was "more" foreign than the other. After

completing a census of North Township on July 30, 1907, Richard Schaaf, Jr., a North Township Trustee, reported that foreign-born residents made up fully 75 percent of the people of East Chicago, and an even greater 85 percent of the population of Indiana Harbor. But East Chicago had a high percentage of the so-called Old Immigration, including Welsh, English, Irish, Scandinavian, and German; the number of nationalities in East Chicago was limited mainly to northern European, Slavic, and Italian, and the number of races to one: white. Polyglot Indiana Harbor, on the other hand, had all of the tongues of Babel and all of the colors of the rainbow, and the number of races and nationalities was unlimited.

All of this is to say that any story about the municipality of East Chicago must be a diptych, two stories in one.

The city's unique twinness often inspired East Chicago and Indiana Harbor theater managers to conduct promotions that had everyone seeing double. Photo from the East Chicago Historical Society

Indiana Harbor and East Chicago once entered separate beauty queens in the Miss America competition. Here is a Miss Indiana Harbor from the pre-bikini era. Photo from the East Chicago Historical Society

The Four Corners of East Chicago was the transfer point for the Green Line trolley. Tracks curving to the left between a park and the Forsyth Block reached Whiting and, ultimately Chicago. Tracks running vertically reached Indiana Harbor in one direction and Hammond in the other. Photo from the East Chicago Historical Society

East Chicago, Ind. *Do you recognize this corner Sam Cohn.*

NASSAU & THOMPSON, PUBLISHERS, EAST CHICAGO, IND.

2699. Chicago Avenue, looking East from Forsyth Avenue

1906

Traditional culture in the Twin City owed its perpetuation mainly to the two women's clubs, which had long histories of upgrading the community's couth. Here the Indiana Harbor Women's Improvement Club is shown meeting at the Fir Street home of the Frank Callahans. This group represents the women behind most of early Indiana Harbor's most energetic shakers and movers. Front row left to right were Mrs. Ernest Summers, Mrs. Ross Myers, unknown, unknown, Miss Ena Meno, Mrs. Lillian Spittle, Miss Emma Hoch, unknown, unknown, and Miss Maud Stevens. Second row were unknown, Mrs. L. C. Weirich, unknown, Mrs. George Witt, unknown, and unknown. First row on porch were Ethel Galvin Marshall, Mrs. A.G. Lundquist, unknown, unknown, unknown, Ann Lewis, next five unknown, Mrs. A. G. Allen, Mrs. Frank Callahan with her daughter Helen in front of her, Mrs. Robert Ansley, and unknown. Top row were first three unknown, Mrs. Enos Drummond, unknown, Mrs. James H. Gardner, unknown, Mrs. Harriet Winslow, and the rest unknown. Photo from the East Chicago Historical Society

East Chicago's first church, a Methodist Episcopal church, organized in 1889, and held its first services in the Tod Opera House. Shortly thereafter, it built a church and parsonage. Indiana Harbor's first church also was a Methodist Episcopal church, which first convened in the Pennsylvania Avenue home of Mrs. Peterson. The twenty-four charter members next rented a nearby meeting hall, known later as the Wigwam Annex to Frank Jerome's furniture store, and held their first service there October 12, 1902. When church members moved southward, the congregation abandoned plans to build a church at the corner of Commonwealth and Michigan avenues, and bought a site at the corner of Grapevine (Grand Boulevard) and 135th streets, where they built the church shown here being dedicated on September 24, 1911. Photo from the East Chicago Historical Society

St. Patrick's began when the Reverend
Thomas Mungovan organized a parish there
in 1902 to serve the eight Catholics who lived
in Indiana Harbor. The parish built a
wooden, two-story combination church,
school, and residence in 1903, and a rectory
in 1905. A new church, school, and parish
hall was built in 1923, and a convent for the
Sisters of the Holy Cross, who were the
school's teachers. The first confirmation class
at the new facility is shown here in 1925.
Father Connelly, a familiar community figure
who served St. Patrick's for several decades,
can be seen on the left as a young man.
Photo from the collection of Nell and Bess
McAuley

St. Stanislaus, founded in 1896 when Father
Kobylinski built and dedicated this modest
wooden church to St. Michael, became one of
the largest parishes in the state. The first
permanent pastor, Father John Kubacki, later
built a school and moved the church to
Baring Avenue, at which time the name was
changed to St. Stanislaus. Saint John Cantius
Church began with the Reverend John
Kubacki's service to the few Poles who lived
in Indiana Harbor in 1903 and when the Rev.
Budnik founded the parish in 1906 and began
to use a two-story stone building for church
and school functions. By 1907, there were
some nine hundred Poles in the parish, and
Father Stachowiak started to build a new
frame rectory. Photo from the East Chicago
Historical Society

ST. STANISLAUS
CATHOLIC CHURCH
EAST CHICAGO

The Carnegie Library in East Chicago, shown here in the 1930s, and its fraternal twin in Indiana Harbor opened on successive days in 1913. Both libraries were subsequently enlarged, the East Chicago library in 1924 and again in 1938, the Indiana Harbor library in 1931 and again a few years later. Both spawned several branch libraries. The East Chicago library recently has been been renovated and renamed the Robert A. Pastrick branch, while the Indiana Harbor library has been succeeded by a building near Sunnyside that serves as main library for the entire library system. The circle in front of the East Chicago library is a remnant of the city's first park, and a memorial to the early park system. Photo from the East Chicago Historical Society

The Tod Opera House Block, built at East Chicago's Four Corners in 1888, was East Chicago's finest building, and served as the community's de facto civic center for almost two decades. It housed stores, traveling road shows, funerals, dances, churches, the East Chicago Company, political rallies, parties, and even East Chicago's first high school. Its counterpart in Indiana Harbor was the Auditorium. Alas, on the morning of March 10, 1907, following a stag party the night before, fire broke out in the building, destroying it; from its rubble eventually arose the more modest Calumet building. The fire, shown here, sorely tested the fire department, recently formalized as a department of city government. It was the first time that the city's new steamer had been called on to pump water substantial distances. Photo from the Edith Wickey Zoeger Collection.

21

East Chicago High School first operated within the Tod Opera House and later, in 1900, in this fortress-like building known as the North Side or Benjamin Harrison School. Indiana Harbor pupils traveled by a rickity trolley to attend classes here until 1914, when the high school took up quarters in Washington School, and East Chicago students traveled to Indiana Harbor to attend it. Photo from the Stuart Thomson Studios

George Washington School in the Park Addition once offered classes from kindergarten through the first year of college. It occupied one city block for classrooms and another city block for athletic grounds. The original building, built in 1908, is seen at the right end of the complex, the east half (1918) in the upper right, the west half (1920) in the upper left, the auditorium and gym (1924) in the center right, and the new wing (1940) in the center left of the complex. Tennis courts to the right of the football field were also used for girls' field hockey and, in the winter, were flooded for day and night community ice skating. Photo from the Stuart Thomson Studios

Theodore Roosevelt School in East Chicago (1924-1925) offered classes from seventh grade through high school. It was added onto in 1929, gained an athletic field that same year, and gained an auditorium and gymnasium in 1936. Its location adjacent to and south of Tod Park, with its lagoons, nine-hole golf course, and Calumet Center of Indiana University (limestone building, center right), gave Roosevelt a campus unlike any other. Not part of the campus were, upper half of photo, the refinery and tanks of Sinclair Oil Company, the west leg of the ship canal, and the tall gas holder (checkerboard top) of the Northern Indiana Public Service Company. Photo from the Stuart Thomson Studios

The Booster Club, shown here in 1907, had its headquarters on Watling Street, and in 1908 evolved into the Commercial Club of Indiana Harbor and East Chicago. Owners of a handsome, commodious clubhouse, recreation center, and eating place on the top floor of 3422-24 Guthrie Street, the Commercial Club was conveniently just a few steps from Indiana Harbor's Four Corners. Club members met every working day for lunch and to exchange information. In 1915, as World War I began to absorb most of the attention of local industry, the club dissolved itself and sold the building to an electrical firm. The clubhouse later became Club Nicholas Iorga, popularly known as the Romanian Club. Photo from the East Chicago Historical Society

Indiana Harbor and East Chicago had separate Boy Scout councils in 1919, with Arthur J. Sambrook, shown here, the executive of the Indiana Harbor Council. A. H. Watts was executive of the East Chicago Council. During the depression of 1921, the two councils united under Sambrook. Photo from the East Chicago Historical Society

Rites of passage were marked by celebrations, as immigrants from a hundred nations all over the world blended their cultures into a unique Twin City culture. In connection with these special days, celebrants often repaired to the favored saloon of their ethnic enclave for respite and a photograph, such as this one taken at John Coman's in the early 1900s. The gathering celebrated a new bride, in all liklihood one sent for from the old country by an older man who had worked in the Twin City long enough to have earned a stake. Photo from the East Chicago Historical Society

The face of Indiana Harbor is this woman's face, which reflects peoples of many lands, uprooted from organic villages and transplanted in a modern, industrial society to do the hard work of the mills and the homes. In 1907, eighty-five percent of all Indiana Harbor residents were foreign-born. That critical mass, with many additional infusions of peoples from elsewhere, has produced one of the strongest, most unique, dynamic communities to be found anywhere. Photo by Tom Hocker

Departed members of ethnic enclaves lay in state at home and, prior to burial, were paraded through the streets of the Twin City, preceded by a band playing a dirge. The corpse and the mourners terminated their melancholy march at the church, where they stopped for a funeral service and the final obligatory photograph. From the East Chicago Historical Society

Black workers recruited by the mills during World War I settled in Indiana Harbor and the Calumet section where they developed comprehensive societies of their own that included institutions dedicated to the spiritual life of their communities. One such group formed the St. Mark A.M.E. Zion Church, founded in 1917, and another the First Baptist Church in the Calumet section in 1918. Officials of the latter church are shown here in a relatively recent photograph; Reverend Hunter is at the lectern. Photo by Tom Hocker

Mexicans in significant numbers first came to Indiana Harbor as strikebreakers during the 1919 Steel Strike. Since that time, they, along with Puerto Ricans, have become the dominant ethnic group in the Twin City. Their big day occurred, and still does, in September, when they celebrated Mexican Independence Day with a parade such as the one shown here. Part of St. Catherine's Hospital can be seen in the background. Photo by Tom Hocker

Following World War II, many displaced persons (DPs) flowed into the Twin City, mostly into Indiana Harbor, where they joined the already large Serbian community of pre-World War I immigrants and their offspring. Here a group of old and new Serbians entertain themselves in the Stepanovich kitchen. That's Dennis Stepanovich to the left, his sister in the middle, and Roger Emig at the right, laughing and holding the goslar. Photo by Tom Hocker

Starting about 1947, Twin City mills sent recruiters to Puerto Rico and returned with contract laborers, who formed into a community within Indiana Harbor that gradually fused with the Mexican community. One of the cultural contributions of Puerto Ricans was the botanica, shown here, a Latino specialty store selling votive candles, incense, powders, magical preparations, fortune-telling books, talismans and other good-luck charms, and assorted devices designed to ward off evil and assure health and happiness. Photo by Tom Hocker

2

THE ELDER TWIN

Belt railroads were critical to the birth and growth of the Twin City. The first was the Chicago and Calumet Terminal Transfer, which was the umbilical cord at the birth of East Chicago. This line apparently sold off pieces of itself in 1896, possibly to the East Chicago Belt, and to the Chicago Terminal Transfer shown here serving Graver Tank. In 1905, the Terminal changed its name to the Indiana Harbor Railroad. Two years later, the East Chicago Belt became the Indiana Harbor Belt and bought properties of the Indiana Harbor Railroad. (By then, the Chicago Junction and the Elgin, Joliet and Eastern also served the Twin City.) Eventually, the Indiana Harbor Belt, with yards at Gibson, owned 125 miles of track, and had rights over the lines of twenty-four railroads in Indiana and thirty-five in Illinois. Because of belt lines, Twin City shippers could tap all trunk lines entering Chicago, and advantageously route their freight quickly at the Chicago rate base. Photo from the East Chicago Historical Society

Before East Chicago

From Eden until 1850, civilization by-passed the Twin City, which was one part sand, three parts water, and no part inhabitable, except by fish and fowl and furry beasties.

As it would always be for many people, the Twin City was primarly a place to work, not live, so hunter Indians came in swarms, worked the rich lowlands, and commuted homeward to comfortable tepees on higher ground.

The solitary break in the calm vegetation of the land occurred when impatient travelers took an overland shortcut to Checagou through the fickle sand of the beach, soft and languid in summer, hard and swift in winter. Eventually, the shortcut became institutionalized as the Detroit-Chicago Road, and when the Illinois and Michigan Canal became more than a rumor, more people than ever traveled the lakeshore fringe of the Twin City until, in 1833, the beach road became a regular stage route. That was the year Hannah Berry built a crude log inn near where Poplar Point (Indiana Harbor) jutted into Lake Michigan. Elsewhere in the land destined to be the Twin City, only the creatures stirred.

But land is what a person dreams it to be, and when George Washington Clarke beheld it he saw the heart of a magnificent city, the equal or better of budding Chicago a few miles to the northwest. A civil engineer, Clarke had arrived in Chicago in 1833 to survey the Illinois and Michigan Canal, which was to have five feeder rivers, one of them the Calumet. So he got to know the territory, and he knew that after the Treaty of Tippecanoe in 1832, whites had begun to move into the high and dry ground of the glacial basin inside the morraine that encircled the southeast corner of Lake Michigan, and that, like the Indians, they had avoided the plaguey swampland nearest the Big Lake. Until 1850.

At mid-century, three events changed settlement preferences. First, a series of crop failures during the 1840s chased thousands of Germans to America, and by 1850 Chicago overflowed with land-hungry Teutonic farmers who began to back up into soggy Lake County, Indiana. Second, in 1850, the federal government ceded all unowned swampland to the respective states to re-sell and reclaim; the Twin City was part of that land. Third, railroads from the East began to slog through the swamps to Chicago, and they hired the resident Germans who, having farmed the edges of sloughs with limited success, supplemented their incomes by working as section hands. This promise of employment attracted other German farmer/gandy dancers to the territory. Whatever few people lived on the sand that stuck up above the water in the pre-Twin City were Germans.

For Clarke, it was time to act. Starting in 1853, he began to buy all the swampland he could afford. In all, he acquired almost twenty thousand acres, selling some of it, but holding onto most, including what became the Twin City. At the same time, Clarke helped George Washington Cass, a shirttail relative, lay his Pittsburgh, Fort Wayne and Chicago Railroad, the Pennsylvania's western leg, diagonally through the new Clarke estate. He did everything possible to make his dream of a metropolis at the foot of Lake Michigan come true. Alas, Clarke's was a fitful dream, frustrated by the Panic of 1857 and the Civil War, and ended by his death in 1866.

Clarke's dream then passed to his brother-in-law, Jacob Forsyth, who already had bought the timber rights to Clarke's estate. A cultured Ulster Scot from Limvady and a prosperous railroad executive, Forsyth bought out Clarke's heirs. He also bought the large frame house and 120-acre farm of Dominick Mutter, a German settler of Poplar Point, and moved his wife and nine children into it. Nearby, Forsyth established a sawmill and several cabins for sawyers. He called the community Cassella, in honor of Cass and his wife, who was Forsyth's cousin. There he began to profitably serve the wood hungry Chicago market, which already had become the lumber capital of the world. All went well until October 8, 1871.

On that day, the day after the Great Chicago Fire, a holocaust drove the Forsyth family into Lake Michigan and reduced Cassella to ashes. But Forsyth refused to quit. He bought the home and sawmill of Louis Ahlendorf near the Grand Calumet River, re-started his lumbering operations, and tried to sell large chunks of his estate. Earlier, Forsyth had sold land around the mouth of the Calumet River to James H. Bowen, who then founded South Chicago nearby and developed five thousand acres of land. That development generated plans for new industry all the way down to and across the state line. Just south of the Wolf River, therefore, Forsyth provided the land for the town of Sheffield. Although the Panic of 1873 killed Sheffield aborning, Forsyth bided his time until 1880 when he sold eight thousand acres to an English agent. For some unknown reason, that plan also collapsed, but the stubborn Forsyth tried again in 1881, this time selling another eight thousand acre package—essentially all of what would become the Twin City—to Charles Beatty Alexander, a New York Lawyer.

Alexander paid a million dollars for the land, one-third down with seven years to pay the balance, the first payment due in 1883. Alexander immediately sold the land to the East Chicago Improvement Company for three times the million dollars he had paid, retaining 42 percent ownership in the new company. The East Chicago Improvement Company in turn sold bonds to British investors, headed by Lord Ronald Ruthven Leslie-Melville, a Scottish peer and London banker. In the economically down year of 1883, however, the East Chicago Improvement Company failed to make its first $100,000 payment, and within a month became the object of a Jacob Forsyth foreclosure.

Alarmed at this turn of events, the British bondholders immediately gave their power of attorney to John Stewart Kennedy, a Scottish immigrant who had become a multi-millionaire in railway supplies and later one of Wall Street's leading bankers. Kennedy contested Forsyth's action in court, arguing that the buyers of the land had been deceived as to the character of the property and had therefore refused to make any further payments. In the foreclosure suit that followed, Kennedy produced leading engineers who alleged that the Twin City land was so low it could not be drained into Lake Michigan, nor could it be used at all unless filled to a higher level. Forsyth countered with a survey of his own that showed levels of from five to eighteen feet above the lake. The suit dragged on for four years.

Meanwhile, in 1885, Kennedy sent his nephew, Robert Elliot Tod, just one year in the country from Scotland, to represent Kennedy on the Twin City site. While on location, Tod met General Joseph Thatcher Torrence, Civil War hero, hero of the Chicago Railroad Riots of 1877, pioneer steel expert, and builder of the first steel mill in the Calumet Region. In 1886, Torrence also established a rolling mill on nearby Hammond property promoted by Marcus M. Towle, Hammond's founder, and his associate, James N. Young. With Towle and Young, Torrence then organized the Chicago and Calumet Terminal Railroad, a belt line that would terminate at about Torrence's mill, in Hammond's extreme northeast corner, right next to the Forsyth land. Apparently Tod persuaded Torrence—or perhaps it was the other way around—to extend the railroad eastward as part of a package deal that would resolve the dispute between Forsyth and Kennedy.

With Tod coordinating local parties, Kennedy in 1887 formed two new companies that combined old interests with new interests. The Standard Steel and Iron Company was formed to develop a one thousand-acre site (expanded to 1,637 acres), roughly East Chicago's southeast quadrant: the area is bounded by Chicago Avenue, 151st Street, Forsyth Avenue, and Railroad Avenue. A second company, the Calumet Canal and Improvement Company, was formed to develop and sell the remainder of the Forsyth land. Owners of the two companies included all of the original principals (Forsyth, Alexander, and Leslie-Melville), plus Kennedy (who by then had invested heavily in the East Chicago project), Towle and Young (chief financiers of the belt railroad), and Torrence. In addition, fresh money came into the development from Eastern and British sources. Torrence headed both companies, as Clarke's dream of a metropolis at the foot of Lake Michigan passed from Forsyth to Alexander to Leslie-Melville to Kennedy to Torrence.

Village: 1888

After surveying the land personally and preparing a plan for its development, Torrence hired Colonel Redmond D. Walsh, a veteran railroad builder, to build the Chicago and Calumet Terminal and prepare the land. This included a fork-shaped ditch that, when completed, was intended to connect Lake Michigan with all inland lakes in the vicinity and the river. Once that was completed, Walsh laid out the streets and, with others, began to erect buildings. The first industrial construction began in the spring of 1888, when William Graver dispatched William H. Penman to East Chicago to build a new Graver Tank Works. Penman broke ground for the new plant on June 14, 1888. Penman's arrival in East Chicago also sparked a housing boom. He built the first single-family, permanent home in the village, locating it convenient to his work on the northwest corner of Tod and 148th Street, cater-corner from the Graver Tank Works. Soon a whole cluster of houses built up around Graver Tank.

Meanwhile, commercial buildings began to spring up at or near the Four Corners: Forsyth and Chicago avenues. John W. Funkhouser, operator of a livery stable, built his barns on the

back end of lots later occupied by the First National Bank. Soon Sam Cohen's saloon went up on the Four Corners, and next door a man named Silverman moved into a combination hardware, restaurant and general store. Nearby, Standard Steel and Iron built its barn on the corner of 145th and Magoun, where an Irish foreman named O'Neil, and later Hugh Rigney, was in charge.

The grandest edifice of all, however, was started in the summer of 1888. The three-story brick Tod Opera House Block, built on the southwest corner of Forsyth and Chicago, was fit for a town twenty times the size of East Chicago, and symbolized its potential. It was to become the principal meeting place of pioneer East Chicagoans, the scene of many happy events. Stores of various types occupied the ground floor. A theater dominated the second floor, in which traveling repertories, such as *Uncle Tom's Cabin*, and churches held services. Rooms on the third floor were used for religious worship, schools, and other gatherings, including spirited political meetings. There would even be a funeral held in Tod Opera House when Robert Ross, super-intendent of the the rolling mill and an active public citizen, died. Not only did the Tod Opera House become a virtual civic center, it non-verbally communicated Torrence's vision of the future. It became the showpiece when Standard Steel and Iron brought prospective buyers in by special trains to evaluate the town site, and fed them free food and beer Sundays at the local park across the street, where maps of the community were distributed.

Before long the village needed a hotel, and on October 27, 1888, John S. Reiland began building one. It was completed and opened on New Year's day, 1889. On that historic occasion, John H. Lesh, who had built a sawmill in the village, symbolically paid a lavish ten dollars for the first breakfast served in the hotel. Within a year there would be two other hotels—The Calumet House at the corner of 149th and Olcott, and the East Chicago Hotel, at Chicago and Olcott. But even with three hotels there was not enough room at the inns for everyone who wished to live in the village. While many of the womenless men lived and boarded at the three hotels, many others roomed and/or boarded in the few private homes of the village, some of the married women in town supplementing their housekeeping allowances by renting rooms in their homes and serving meals. As the population grew rapidly, stores appeared in rapid succession. Colonel Funkhouser was the first storekeeper in town, opening a grocery store on November 8, 1888, and selling the first piece of cheese to Mrs. Brennell.

Close on the heels of people came the institutions, the three most important being the school, the church, and the saloon. On November 16, 1888, the first school term started with Miss Eliza "Lizzie" Brennell teaching thirteen pupils in a small cottage that Torrence had the Standard Steel and Iron Company build for the purpose. The land company also paid for all the furniture, books, and even the teacher's salary. On November 18, 1888, The Reverend R. C. Wall of the St. Mary's Episcopal Mission in East Chicago organized a Sunday School, preached the first sermon, and gave the first service. As for the first saloon, it is not possible to date its appearance, although it is probable that this dispenser of social and spiritual sustenance preceded the institutions of school and church. In any case, the first saloonkeeper to be granted a license was Anson H. Smith, proprietor of the East Chicago Hotel and, in 1890, a councilman. He paid a town license of one hundred dollars per year and had to religiously observe a seven o'clock nightly closing.

After the three basic institutions became established, the village quickly began to take on the characteristics of a town, as stores and services appeared. In December, 1888, Fred J. Fife became the first non-grocery merchant in East Chicago, opening a men's clothing store. Harry Cohen closely followed Fife with a shoe and boot store at the corner of Olcott and 148th. By the end of 1888, East Chicago's outlines were well defined and buildings were going up at a rapid rate. But while the village began to look like a town, it scarcely functioned like one. As the new year of 1889 began, there were no electric lights, no water works, no gas for the thousand or so people in the village, and the only means of transportation in or out of the remote community was a branch of the Pennsylvania Railroad. Within the village, land was so swampy that villagers could not walk far from the industrial core without hip boots. Sand streets stretched southward to 151st Street, but there was not much north of Chicago Avenue, and east of Railroad Avenue a virgin wilderness served as home for an abundance of wild animals. In fact, before Colonel Walsh eventually got around to leveling and filling beyond the original 160 acres, the men of the village spent their evenings hunting wolves in the surrounding ridge and slough country.

George Washington Clarke sailed a boatload of portable homes around Cape Horn, sold them to Forty Niners in the California gold fields, and used the proceeds to buy some twenty thousand acres of Calumet Region swampland, including all of what became the Twin City. Photo from the Historical Encyclopedia of Illinois

Jacob Forsyth, a native of Northern Ireland, established the first settlement in the Twin City in 1867, a sawmill community he called Cassella in what became Indiana Harbor. It was destroyed in 1871 by a holocaust, but Forsyth persisted in the development of all of his land, and his persistence resulted in the creation of the village of East Chicago in 1888. Photo from the Chicago Historical Society

George Washington Cass, along with Jacob Forsyth, probably underwrote Clarke in his swampland venture, and may have later backed Forsyth in his attempts to capitalize on the land. With Clarke doing the surveying, Cass built the trunkline of the Pittsburgh, Fort Wayne and Chicago Railroad diagonally through the Clarke/Forsyth estate right past Forsyth's sawmill, and ran a branch of the line through what became the village of East Chicago. Sketch by Andrew J. Biancardi

Charles Beatty Alexander, who in 1881 paid Jacob Forsyth one million dollars for what became East Chicago, Indiana, served as junior counsel to Samuel Tilden during hearings to break the tie in the Presidential election of 1876 between Tilden and Rutherford Hayes. In 1888, Alexander married Harriet Crocker, daughter of Charles, one of the Big Four who built the Central Pacific Railroad, the western half of the nation's first transcontinental railroad. The Alexanders became one of New York's most prominent families, and he became a New York state regent. Alexander Hall at Princeton University is named for Charles Beatty Alexander. Photo from the Princeton University Archives

John Stewart Kennedy after 1892 controlled the East Chicago Improvement Company. A native of Scotland, Kennedy emigrated to America and made a fortune in railroad supplies and banking. He was an incorporator of the Union Pacific Railroad, the eastern half of the first transcontinental railroad, and financed many western railroads, including the Canadian Pacific Railway and James J. Hill's Great Northern system, the only transcontinental railroad built exclusively with private funds. Kennedy also became one of the great philanthropists of the nineteenth and early twentieth centuries, and was instrumental in creating a library in New York. The bust of Kennedy shown here resides in the New York Public Library and was created by the renowned sculptor, Hermon Atkins MacNeil. Photo from the Art, Prints, Photograph Division, The New York Public Library, Astor, Lenox and Tilden Foundations

Robert Elliot Tod became the putative founder of East Chicago when he brought all disputants over the Forsyth land together in a compromise. Like his patron and uncle, John Stewart Kennedy, Tod emigrated from Scotland to America to make his fortune. After one year at Princeton, he went west as an eighteen-year-old to represent his uncle in the East Chicago flap. As a tribute to his success, Tod Opera House was named for him, and Tod Avenue and Tod Park, East Chicago's largest, still bear his name. After leaving East Chicago, Tod became one of the world's most famous yachtsmen and helped defend the America's Cup. He was also a decorated World War I hero, and commissioner of immigration at Ellis Island at a time, ironically, when many of East Chicago's citizens passed through its facilities. From the Anne Johnston Collection

General Joseph Thatcher Torrence, planner and developer of East Chicago, in 1887 became president of the two land companies that resulted from John Stewart Kennedy's reconstituted investment syndicate. He designed and laid out the original townsite, including the great forked ditch that thirteen years later became the Calumet Canal, a.k.a. Indiana Harbor Ship Canal. In 1890, Torrence was deposed as head of the two East Chicago land companies when he refused to sell land in what became Indiana Harbor, while focusing all of his attention on rapidly-developing East Chicago. A hero of both the Civil War and the Railroad Riots of 1877, Torrence was also one of the nation's first true steel experts. Photo from the Chicago Historical Society

George Calvin Magoun represented two important sources of investment money in the Kennedy-reconstituted syndicate that brought East Chicago into existence. He was a partner in the Boston-based investment firm of Kidder Peabody and Company, and he was also a partner with Thomas Baring in Baring and Magoun, Baring being a member of the family that owned the great merchant bank, Baring Brothers. (Thomas Baring was one of three Barings involved in the creation of East Chicago. His brother Cecil became a partner in Kidder, Peabody and Company, New York, a.k.a. Baring and Magoun, and Alexander Baring became a partner in J. Kennedy-Tod.) Magoun also served as chairman of the Atchison, Topeka, and the Santa Fe Railroad. One of Magoun's sons married the daughter of East Chicago's architect, Kinsley Magoun marrying General Torrence's daughter, Jessie. Sketch by Andrew J. Biancardi

Colonel John J. McCook, one of the famous "Fighting McCooks" of Civil War fame, was connected with the East Chicago project in a variety of ways. He was attorney for both Kidder Peabody and Company and the Atchison, Topeka, and the Santa Fe Railroad; he was a member of the same Civil War company of Ohio volunteers as Joseph Thatcher Torrence; and he was Charles Beatty Alexander's brother-in-law. He ultimately bought at auction the Chicago Horseshoe Company, one of the first industries to build in East Chicago. The town of McCook, Illinois, is named in his honor. Sketch by Andrew J. Biancardi

Mulepower not only built East Chicago, but symbolized the persistence of its first citizens. The redoubtable Colonel Walsh used twenty-seven-mule teams to drag slough scrapers, road scrapers, wagons, tracklaying equipment, and a gaudy collection of other equipment through the mucky and sandy terrain. He bought the mules from Jacob Forsyth, a tenacious Ulster Scot, who raised and sold them on his Sheffield farm. When Walsh decided the mules were not worth what Forsyth charged for them, the two most stubborn men in East Chicago's history sought satisfaction in court, and they carried their fight to the highest court with jurisdiction. In the end, Forsyth wound up having to pay Walsh six hundred dollars in costs in a fight over mules that were worth ten dollars. *From the East Chicago Historical Society*

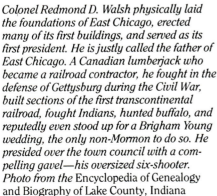

Colonel Redmond D. Walsh physically laid the foundations of East Chicago, erected many of its first buildings, and served as its first president. He is justly called the father of East Chicago. A Canadian lumberjack who became a railroad contractor, he fought in the defense of Gettysburg during the Civil War, built sections of the first transcontinental railroad, fought Indians, hunted buffalo, and reputedly even stood up for a Brigham Young wedding, the only non-Mormon to do so. He presided over the town council with a compelling gavel—his oversized six-shooter. *Photo from the* Encyclopedia of Genealogy and Biography of Lake County, Indiana

The first building erected in East Chicago was the Forsyth Block, shown here at the right, at a time when East Chicago was macadamizing its main roads. It was situated on the northeast corner of Forsyth and Chicago avenues, and was built by George Neer, whose wife was the first woman to live in East Chicago. As the only residential building in the village for a while, it housed many of the people who built the town, as well as a drug store and the only physician in town. Notice the station of the Pittsburgh, Fort Wayne, and Chicago Railroad in the background. Recently modernized, it serves today as the office of East Chicago's mayor. *From the East Chicago Historical Society*

William H. Penman became East Chicago's first mayor in 1893, the year the community attained city status. He had come to East Chicago in 1888 to supervise construction of the Graver plant in East Chicago, and stayed on to superintend the plant and become active in public affairs. He served as town treasurer in 1889, but quit within a few months in a dispute with Colonel Walsh, a financial conservative, on the issue of internal improvements. When he became mayor of the new city, he led an internal improvement spree that eventually led to the bankruptcy of East Chicago's utilities. From the East Chicago Historical Society

Fred J. Fife opened a men's clothing store in December, 1888, the first non-grocery store in the new village of East Chicago. A Canadian who followed his uncle, Colonel Walsh, to East Chicago, Fife began as a bookkeeper for the Chicago and Calumet Terminal. He was given the honor of turning over the first shovelful of dirt for what would be the Four Corners, the intersection of Forsyth and Chicago avenues. From the East Chicago Historical Society

Irwin and Hascall Lumber Yards, shown here, was an extension of the pioneer East Chicago industry, Lesh, Prouty & Abbott, head-quartered in Goshen; Fred Hascall ran the office and finances in East Chicago. The mill was the only one in the United States devoted exclusively to the manufacture of black walnut, and it exported its products internationally through distribution points in major cities of the world. All wood run through the mill was from hardwood logs shipped in by rail from central Indiana. Lesh Hascall, a 1904 graduate of East Chicago High School and an army captain in France during World War I, organized the high school's first baseball team and pitched in the first game. From the East Chicago Historical Society

Town: 1889

With the break of spring, civilization began to push out from the center of the village, and the residents decided it was time to have a town. In March, 1889, the Lake County Board of Commissioners approved the village's request for incorporation, and on March 30, the citizens elected governing trustees: Colonel Walsh, John M. Brennell, and Martin Lehmann. They took office May 6, and elected Colonel Walsh president. The new Trustees then appointed other town officials: Armanis F. Knotts and Wilbur Reading, attorneys; William H. Penman, treasurer; James J. Reynolds, civil engineer; Frederick J. Fife, clerk; John W. Funkhouser, fire marshal; and Neil Patterson, marshal.

The new town of about three and three-quarter square miles began well. General Torrence immediately donated to the new town a fire department site, and since the original school house had become too small, he moved it to a site designated for a town hall. But government crawled, slowed by the redoubtable Colonel Walsh, who opposed what he considered to be lavish expenditures of public funds that didn't exist in the first place. Time after time he influenced other trustees to take a conservative course, gaveling down liberal propositions with his oversized six-shooter. Finally William Penman quit in disgust, and Frank Clinton, the grocer, replaced him.

Throughout 1889, the new town grew in all directions, and as it expanded, the men willingly fulfilled their legal duties as citizens to work a prescribed amount of time on public projects, like creating ditches and roads and even the belt railroad that was crucial to East Chicago's success. Those who were unable or unwilling to contribute their sweat in civic enterprises could hire a substitute—which is to say pay taxes—this being the last refuge of a nineteenth-century East Chicagoan who shirked his civic duties. Despite all of the free citizen labor available to the town, though, demand for services continued to grow as the population grew. With the little school cottage too cramped to house the number of children requiring an education, Herman Hirsch, editor of the East Chicago *Journal*, the town's first newspaper, turned to the township for action. On July 30, 1889, he editorialized:

> The proper officials who have charge of our township for schools should look out for our little ones' interests. We have nearly 200 children running around the street, and provision must be at once made. Let the disgrace not fall upon the State of Indiana that people should say, "Here is the model town of East Chicago with 1,200 inhabitants and no school."

While town leaders struggled with East Chicago's growing pains, industries in the Standard Steel and Iron plot grew in number, coming in steady procession, drawn by comparatively inexpensive lots and low taxes, and for a variety of other reasons, such as proximity and access to markets. Graver Tank was the first plant completed. By October, 1889, in fact, Graver Tank Works teemed with seventy-five employees, and was already planning for expansion. As industries like Graver and others completed their buildings and began operating, the town filled out and the institutions came faster than ever, especially the churches and saloons. The more the town grew the more the pressure increased for services, which sometimes were provided in unexpected ways.

Andrew Wickey, an inventor and manufacturer of farm machinery, decided one day to electrify his home. So he installed a generator at his plant, the Famous Manufacturing Company, and ran wires to his house a few blocks away, at 145th and Olcott. When his makeshift system worked, Wickey's house at first became a community amusement but ultimately, the envy of his neighbors. In an act of consummate public service, Wickey added enough generators to light the whole town, and the denizens demonstrated a pioneer willingness to tolerate inconvenience so as to be in step with the march of progress. Whenever East Chicago's first electrical system malfunctioned, Wickey blew the plant whistle, and a paralyzed community began to count and gird itself for bad news. One long blast merely meant an interruption of power. Two signaled minor trouble. Three meant serious trouble. After a count of three, the women of the community automatically got out kerosene lamps and prepared for a long evening of semi-darkness.

Not everything worked so well. After Walsh finished the digging of the forked ditch, Torrence presented it as a gift to the federal government, assuming the government would complete and maintain it. The government declined the gift. So Torrence stopped construction of the canal, and transferred all of his considerable energies to development of the booming Standard Steel and Iron plot. With proceeds from the sale of lots in the Standard Steel and Iron plot, Torrence reduced the debt incurred to finance the belt railroad. Meanwhile, he sat on the land nearest Lake Michigan, which greatly vexed the British bondholders, especially Baring Brothers, one of the world's largest banks, and England's *de facto* federal reserve system.

As a result of poor railroad investments in South America, Barings had experienced such a severe shortage of funds that it had called in all of its cash worldwide, and liquidated whatever assets it could. Since part of Barings' assets lay idle in land Torrence sat on while he practically minted money in East Chicago, Barings accused Torrence through Kennedy of willful neglect, and demanded his scalp. In the hysteria of what came to be called the Baring Panic of 1890, Kennedy sent Robert Elliot Tod, by then a New York resident and a partner in J. Kennedy-Tod, back to East Chicago to seek Torrence's resignation as president of both the Standard Steel and Iron Company and the Calumet Canal and Improvement Company. The issue was painfully resolved when Torrence agreed to withdraw and turn his attention to another of his visionary projects, the elevation of all railroad tracks entering Chicago. By 1892, both Torrence and Forsyth had divested themselves of their stock in the two East Chicago land companies, selling or trading (for land, in Forsyth's case) to J. Kennedy-Tod, which thus gained controlling interest in the East Chicago Improvement Company.

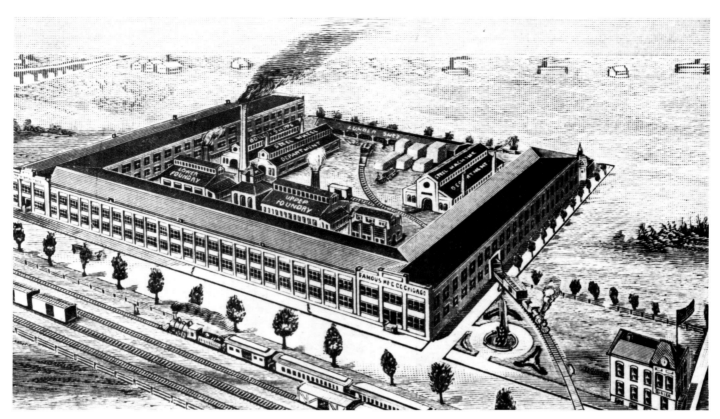

The Famous Manufacturing Company was established in East Chicago in 1889 by German-born Andrew Wickey. It produced hay bailers and other farm equipment, producing more presses than any other factory in the world. This plant also served as East Chicago's first electric light power plant. Famous later also produced the only automobiles ever made in East Chicago, high-wheel roadsters favored by physicians, farmers, or anyone else who did most of their driving on the rutty, muddy, rural roads of the early twentieth century. Drawing from the East Chicago Historical Society

City: 1893

During the time Torrence and Forsyth were withdrawing, Torrence's well-conceived East Chicago continued to boom. The community grew to such an extent, in fact, that the town became a city, and on March 14, 1893, voters elected East Chicago's first city officers and councilmen. The mayor was William H. Penman, the treasurer, Frank W. Clinton, the clerk, Edwin S. Gilbert. The first council consisted of Robert Ross, John M. White, Jule C. Pepin, Edward S. Yaste, William J. Glover, and Louis Loucks. Free of Colonel Walsh's constraints, the exuberant council also authorized and equipped a fire department, a municipally-owned water system, and even a city electrical system, all located near the City Hall, the erstwhile school house.

The new city also had a judicial branch, with Byron M. Cheney serving as the first justice of the peace in East Chicago. Cheney became widely famous for the informality of his court. Not one to endure heat gladly, Cheney held court on his lawn during the dog days of summer and became known in Chicago newspapers as the "out-of-doors-court-judge." The practice ended when Cheney's wife, who ran a boarding house, overturned the al fresco court. She didn't mind the spectacle, but she couldn't tolerate court hangers-on ruining her lawn.

These were the salad days of East Chicago's youth. They didn't last long. Within months of the euphoria of new cityhood, the chain reaction set off by the Baring Panic culminated in the Panic of 1893, which was followed by the worst economic depression in the nation's history to that point. Not only did the hard times almost bankrupt the new city, they paralyzed industrial development and gradually atrophied it. Ironically, the panic and depression even froze the sale and development of Calumet Canal and Improvement Company land. Yet for all of its devastation, the Panic of 1893 and the long depression it intro-duced affected East Chicago positively, in a negative way.

The panic and depression had staggered, but not immediately knocked out East Chicago's leading employer, the National Forge and Iron Company. When the company finally had to cut wages in 1894, however, workers greeted the cut with a strike, and half of the company's workforce went out. The strike killed the rolling mill. In the next three years, the company passed through a succession of receivers, and finally wound up on the sheriff's block in 1897. The auction revolutionized the history of East Chicago, and led to the creation of a Twin City.

The winning bidder for the old rolling mill was Philip D. Block, of the four-year-old Inland Steel Company. He bought the assets of East Chicago's largest employer for fifty thousand dollars and then engineered an extraordinary deal with the city that benefited both parties. In exchange for a promise to reopen the plant in East Chicago, Block received free water and a waiver of all taxes for a half century. As a sweetener, he also received from the Standard Steel and Iron Company several acres of valuable land. His action inspired the land company to proclaim that revival of the rolling mill would attract three new factories to the city, and it did.

Under the direction of Leopold Block, Philip's brother, the re-named Inland Iron and Forge quadrupled furnace capacity within two years, and became profitable. But fierce competition in the post-panic nineties had made consolidation the standard survival strategem in the iron and steel industry, and Inland had to decide whether to stay in the business and fight it out

with super corporations, or sell to one of the large consolidations. Fortunately, while Inland pondered that question, another East Chicago story was coming to a climax that would give Inland the answer.

As the economy began to show early signs of recovery, Tod, who had replaced Torrence as head of the two land development companies, had been able to attract two major investors to the land adjacent to Lake Michigan. One sale was to a man who sat on several boards with Uncle John Kennedy, Henry Clay Frick, the coke king and Andrew Carnegie's chief lieutenant. Tod sold him three hundred acres on the northwest bank of the proposed harbor and canal. On the opposite side of the phantom harbor and canal, Tod sold several hundred acres to the Lake Michigan Land Company, whose head was another Kennedy associate, Owen Franklin Aldis. The Lake Michigan Land Company itself was the product of the fertile mind of Albert De Wolfe Erskine, Tod's western sales manager, and also included such prestigious people as Potter Palmer, Jr., scion of Chicago's most famous family. Before the end of the century, the Lake Michigan Land Company owned thirteen hundred acres southeast of the proposed canal. All that remained was for the harbor and canal to be built.

Faced with the problem of needing a waterway to attract industry but needing industry to justify the waterway, Erskine offered to give away part of the land, while keeping a string attached to it. Specifically, he offered the Block brothers and Inland Steel fifty acres of free land at Poplar Point, provided Inland build a million dollar open-hearth steel plant there. The Blocks agreed on the condition that Erskine guarantee that a harbor and belt railroad be built to service the plant. Without having the vaguest idea of how that would be accomplished, Erskine made the dual transportation system a condition of sale.

To finance most of the new plant, the Blocks sold the rolling mill to the new Republic Iron and Steel Company for stock in that company, and then sold the Republic stock. Meanwhile, Erskine told Tod and Frick that he was sure he could attract a steel mill to Poplar Point provided they stop waiting for promises from governments at various levels, and finance the waterway with their own funds. They agreed to pay for sixty percent. Erskine then passed that word along to the Blocks who, already too deep in the Poplar Point morass to back out, agreed to pick up the rest. They insisted, however, that a built-up town for their workers to live in be thrown in with the canal and belt railroad. Erskine then transmitted this additional condition to Aldis and persuaded him and the Lake Michigan Land Company to create an entirely new town from scratch. Stuck in the Poplar Point quagmire himself, Aldis reluctantly agreed. Thus, in 1901, construction of a harbor, canal, steel mill, and new city began.

First officials of the new city of East Chicago, shown here front row, left to right, were Byron Cheney, justice of the peace; John M. White, alderman; Robert Ross, alderman; William H. Penman, mayor; Louis T. Loucks, alderman; and Jule C. Pepin, alderman. In the back row were Edwin S. Gilbert, clerk; Frank W. Clinton, treasurer; Neil Patterson, police chief; and E. S. Yaste, alderman. Photo from the Edith Wickey Zoeger Collection

Edwin S. Gilbert, shown here in the doorway next to Town Marshall Neil Patterson, published in 1891 the first newspaper to be printed in East Chicago. He called it the East Chicago Globe, an allusion to the community's cosmopolitan view. Gilbert also was elected East Chicago's first city clerk in 1893, published the Whiting News, was Indiana Harbor's first postmaster in 1902, and published that community's first newspaper, the Indiana Harbor News. Photo from the East Chicago Historical Society

41

A formal volunteer fire department, organized in 1893, soon could boast this fancy fire truck. After the turn of the century the department even had a steam kettle, a hose cart, and a separate buggy for the chief. The first fire chief was John Funkhouser, probably the man holding the lantern. The man in the photo with a star on his chest is Neil Patterson, the town marshal who became the new city's first police chief. Issac Specter may be the fire laddie blowing the horn. The cottage in the background is East Chicago's first schoolhouse, which was moved to space reserved for the City Hall and, in fact, served as City Hall for more than fifteen years. When East Chicago got around to paying for this fire protection, it applied a piece rate: five dollars per fire for firefighters, and ten dollars per fire for the chief. Photo from the East Chicago Historical Society

Five daughters of Hammond's Holmes family shown here married five East Chicago men. Left to right were Emma M. Smith (C. C.'s wife), Dora Merrifield, Edith Miller, Nellie Jacobson, and Lucia Jackson. Two of Edith Miller's children managed two of East Chicago's most essential utilities; Bruce Miller became superintendent of the water department, and Golda Miller ran the Chicago Avenue Chocolate Shop. Photo from the Roland H. Smith Collection

Edward W. Wickey became city attorney in 1894, shortly after East Chicago gained city status. He was elected by the common council, and succeeded Wilbur Reading who, along with A. F. Knotts, had been attorney from the time East Chicago gained town status. Son of Andrew, Edward Wickey distinguished himself as a forceful speaker and an extremely effective litigator. Beyond the city's limits, Wickey was the best-known of all East Chicagoans. Photo from the East Chicago Historical Society

June 16 1896

East Chicago High School's first students shown here had a decidedly female bias. Front row, left to right were Professor J. M. Wood, science teacher and first principal; Miss Bronson, English teacher; Miss Toms, German teacher; Robert Ross, Township Trustee (North Township controlled public schools at that time); Eugene Merriman, eighth grade teacher, principal, and eventually superintendent; and Lucy Bird, a student. In the back row were unknown; unknown; Blanche Stewart Lewis; unknown; Maude Hollingshead (in dark jacket); Lillie Wickey Francis, who died in 1986 at the age of 107; Alice Williams (Mrs. Bert Wickey); Lola Funkhouser Ross; unknown; and unknown. Photo from the Edith Wickey Zoeger Collection

East Chicago's oldest school with a proper building is McKinley School, an early class of which is shown here. Before the McKinley building, pupils attended classes in a two-room cottage and then rooms in the Tod Opera House. Finally, in 1892, the exploding child population of East Chicago moved into the South Side School, a.k.a. Magoun Avenue School. By 1895, there were five hundred pupils enrolled under ten teachers, and when the school building was doubled in size, it was named for President William McKinley, who had come into office during the expansion of the building. Like the President who was shot and killed by an anarchist in 1901, however, the first McKinley School building's existence ended abruptly, a fire wiping it out in 1905. Quickly rebuilt that same year, McKinley School gained an addition in 1910 and a second addition in 1914. An entirely new building was erected in partial response to the baby boom that followed World War II. Other early schools west of the canal were: Berry Lake (about 1896), Benjamin Harrison (1900), and Steiglitz (1901). Early Twin City schools east of the canal were: Wallace (1902), Watling Street (1902), Lincoln (1903), Field (1905), and Washington (1908). Photo from the Edith Wickey Zoeger Collection

East Chicago High School students continued to be predominantly female well after the turn of the century, as boys started in the mills at a young age. In this photo taken at the new Harrison School in 1903, the girls outnumber the boys by about three to one. This class was a pool from which community leaders were drawn following World War I. Front row left to right were Mrs. Bloom, science teacher, Grace Clinton (Eady); Kate Smith, Thomas Riley, Bob Merton, Mary Belle Stirling (McCready), Lora Weydert Parsons, Hazel Cherry, James Ormand, Lottie Donovan, Anna Hiler, Margaret Doggett, Ethel Hand (Peterson), Thomas Henry, Melvin Hascall, Lucy Doggett, Alice Williams, Anna Laura Cole, Mary Reece (Billeter), Miss Lyons, English and history teacher, Miss Sheets, commercial course teacher, and Mr. Smith, superintendent. In the second row were Mr. Slocumb, principal and mathematics teacher; Miss Bronson/Mrs. Johnson, German and Latin teacher; Edith Evans; Charles McKelvey; Gertrude Jacobson; Annie Peterson; Annie Edmunds; Agnes Reed; and Myrtle Spaulding. In the third row were Margaret Saunders, Kathryn McGrath, Garnet Hilty, Ruth Thomas (Van Horne), Sadie Cohen, Elizabeth Jones (Merriam), Annie Peterson, Mary Lightbody, Helen Galvin, Mable Wickey, and Edith Wickey (Zoeger). In the back row were Milton Given, Isadore Jacobson, Laura Wistrand, Maria Stirling, May Barnes, Grace Moss (Loucks), Ella Sheets, Lesh Hascall, Sam Bird, Frank Williams, Effie DeBriae (Hough), Blanche McKelvey (Walsh), Thomas Davis, Henrietta Cole (Havill), Helen Harris (Montgomery), and Vern Weydert. Photo from the Edith Wickey Zoeger Collection

As soon as East Chicago High School had enough boys of reasonably appropriate height, it fielded a basketball team. Prior to 1914, however, the school did not have organized sports and the team played on a club basis. Arden B. Cole, a teacher of mathematics, oversaw the roundballers, and he is shown here with the 1912 team. Photo from the East Chicago Historical Society

William F. Hale, born in Canada in 1866, became clerk of East Chicago in 1896 and mayor in 1898, an office he held until 1906, when he was succeeded by Edward DeBriae. He also founded the Elks in East Chicago. In business, he was a partner with C. D. Moon in the sale of wood, coal, ice, and building materials. William Hale was the elder of a mayoral brother act; Raleigh P. Hale, M.D., served as East Chicago's mayor from 1926 to 1930. Photo from A Standard History of Lake County, Indiana and the Calumet Region

East Chicago's Bloomer Girls were an outgrowth of a gymnastics class started in 1913. This basketball team, East Chicago's first girl's team, was dedicated to developing strong bodies to go with strong minds. Photo from the East Chicago Historical Society

Leopold E. Block, a partner in the Pittsburgh firm of Dreyfuss, Block and Company, was recalled by his father, Joseph, to run the Inland Iron and Forge Company. Within two years, he resurrected the rolling mill so completely that he was able to advantageously sell it to the newly-organized Republic Iron and Steel Company for stock in Republic. He subsequently sold the Republic stock on the New York Curb Exchange for approximately a half-million dollars, which became the substantial down payment on a new open-hearth steel plant in Indiana Harbor. Photo from the East Chicago Historical Society

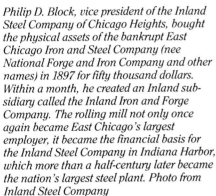

Philip D. Block, vice president of the Inland Steel Company of Chicago Heights, bought the physical assets of the bankrupt East Chicago Iron and Steel Company (nee National Forge and Iron Company and other names) in 1897 for fifty thousand dollars. Within a month, he created an Inland subsidiary called the Inland Iron and Forge Company. The rolling mill not only once again became East Chicago's largest employer, it became the financial basis for the Inland Steel Company in Indiana Harbor, which more than a half-century later became the nation's largest steel plant. Photo from Inland Steel Company

The Inland Iron and Forge Company, shown here, produced a wide variety of products, and employed a high percentage of skilled and semi-skilled workers. After Inland sold the plant to Republic Iron and Steel in 1899, the new owners narrowed the plant's line mainly to iron and steel bars, the making of which required proportionately fewer skilled and semi-skilled workers. This opened opportunities for foreign-born unskilled workers, who poured into East Chicago from Chicago in great numbers. Photo from the Inland Steel Company

Rapid growth of East Chicago's population resulted in part from the increase in the size of immigrant families. The Boudis, shown here, married in Romania where two of their children were born. The father then emigrated to East Chicago, where he found work. To finance the trip to join her husband, Mrs. Boudi sold her papers to another girl in the village and traveled as a stowaway. The Boudis then resumed their family, and, as these two photos illustrate, not only contributed to the growth of East Chicago's population by infusion, but by natural increase. Photos from the Florence Ballentine Collection

One immigrant family in East Chicago often served as a magnet for many others of the same nationality. After the Stiglitz family, shown here, arrived in East Chicago from Zagreb, Croatia, they operated a combination restaurant-tavern-boardinghouse near the mills at Railroad and Emlyn avenues. To staff Stiglitz Tavern, the Stiglitzes brought over to East Chicago many other Croatians who worked in the tavern as de facto indentured servants. Slowly, some of these Croatians and their families fused with other nationalities. Julie Stiglitz, the girl on the extreme left, married a Polish boy named Pete Rucinski, East Chicago's sainted football coach. Photo from the Florence Ballentine Collection

Saloons were among East Chicago's most important social institutions, where neighbors relaxed and relationships often became longstanding. Here neighbors in the Polish quadrant of East Chicago pose on a boardwalk in front of a favored saloon at 5003 Northcote. The girl in the front, left of center, is Ann Mysliwy and the boy in the suspenders, to the far left, is her brother John. Behind John and wearing a vest is Peter Janicki. The man holding the baby may be Anthony Rucinski, father of Pete Rucinski. The blonde girl in the front is Mary Krause, and the girl to her left is Mary Janicki, who got her surname by marrying the boy in the suspenders to become Mrs. John Mysliwy. The tall young man in the vest is someone named Hap, who grew up to work in the bank. Photo from the Sophie Kempski Collection

Life was comfortable for those who lived in the northwest quadrant of East Chicago. Shown here at 4508 Magoun Avenue, some barely discernible, were Edith G. Wickey, Mae Lewis and Mrs. Lewis, Zilah Ineley, Wesley Wickey, Charley Haight, Mable Wickey, and Trix, the clever pet dog. Photo from the Edith Wickey Zoeger Collection

Promotion of business often took the form of gaudily decorated, horsedrawn vehicles that moved through the streets of East Chicago as mobile billboards. In this photo of the Manhattan Lumber and Coal Company's contribution to popular culture, notice the recreation spas in the background—Berry's Theater sandwiched between two saloons. Photo from the East Chicago Historical Society

J. H. Patrick & Son, located on the boardwalk of Olcott Avenue, was one of several sheet metal shops that prospered with the rapid growth of East Chicago and the development of central heating. One of these shops evolved into Gannon Metal Fabricators & Erectors, Inc., still one of the Twin City's important industries. Photo from the Stuart R. Thomson Studios

An Interstate Iron & Steel crew is shown here within the mill that once employed more workers (1,350) than any mill on the west side of the canal. Interstate succeeded Emlyn Iron Works, begun in 1900, and was owned by a Welsh family named Llewelyn. Interstate never fully recovered from the 1921 depression and closed shortly thereafter. Photo from the Stuart R. Thomson Studios

51

Stylish young men in East Chicago found all the fashions they could afford on Olcott Avenue, East Chicago's answer to Fifth Avenue. From the East Chicago Historical Society

Walking great distances along railroad tracks was a popular recreation of early East Chicagoans. In a land of sand ridges interdicted by sloughs, railroad tracks offered the only sure pathway between communities. Photo from the East Chicago Historical Society

Charles Nassau

Charles Nassau and Henry G. Thompson gave up bartending in 1902 and bought East Chicago's only newsstand from Edward Jenkins, water company superintendent. The partners quickly moved the business from Doctor Spear's drug store in the Forsyth Block, across the street to temporary space in the rear of Max Nassau's jewelry store. They then moved into a small shack, where, during the winter of 1902-1903, they dispensed the first ice cream sold in Lake County. After nine

Henry G. Thompson

years, they moved to the Friedman Building and, after disposing of the ice cream business in 1920, moved in 1922 into their new building at 812 Chicago Avenue. After operating on Chicago Avenue for more than eighty-five years, the business still includes the news distributorship, and thrives under the direction of a fourth generation Nassau. Photos from the East Chicago Chamber of Commerce

Robbie Darrow and Frank Ott pause on the boardwalk in front of a typical East Chicago home in 1904. Photo from the Edith Wickey Zoeger Collection

Ice delivered in twenty-five, fifty, seventy-five and one hundred pound chunks slowed the spoilage of food in East Chicago homes during the first third of the twentieth century. Photo from the East Chicago Historical Society

East Chicago Ball Park housed many legendary baseball games including one in 1917 between the married men and single men of Graver Tank. H. Swanson and H. Algrin pitched, as the married men won. The man center front with his arms folded may be Mike Oswego, whose family operated a famous boxing arena on the northeast corner of today's Columbus Drive and Indianapolis Boulevard. Photo from the Stuart Thomson Studios

Rally Day at the Congregational Church was one of the big events of the year. After Sunday School, the entire congregation paraded through the city. Photo from the East Chicago Historical Society

The latest early-century fashions in East Chicago featured plumed hats, yards of fabric, fur coats, and mufflers that were long strings of beads. And one of the best places to display the fashions was in a gaily-decorated dogcart pulled by a well-brushed jackass. Photos from the East Chicago Historical Society

Early East Chicago had two celebrated
citizens named George Lewis. George W.
Lewis, left, joined the two East Chicago land
companies in 1892 as the resident manager.
When all local land companies were consoli-
dated into the East Chicago Company after
the turn of the century, Lewis became its
secretary. He held that office until he resigned
in 1905 to go into the real estate and
insurance business for himself, and generally
become one of the steadiest pillars of the
community. George H. Lewis, right, served
briefly as mayor 1933-34, but is best known as
the co-architect of the East Chicago bill.
When East Chicago's first high school building, started in 1898 and finished in 1900, was
only basement high, the Supreme Court of
Indiana ruled that the school city and the
civic city were one in the matter of bonded
debt. Since the civic city of East Chicago had
already exceeded its borrowing limit, the
school city had no way to raise money to
finish the building, and construction of the
school stopped. Resourcefully, Lewis and
William Jeppeson arranged for a bill, perhaps
still on the books, which allowed cities to
exceed their debt limits, provided their
populations were between 3,410 and 3,420.
East Chicago's population in 1900 was 3,411.
Photos from the East Chicago Historical
Society and the East Chicago Chamber of
Commerce

Moses Specter, shown here, was city treasurer
in 1902, city clerk in 1904, and, upon
appointment by President Theodore
Roosevelt, postmaster in 1907; reappointed by
President William Howard Taft, Specter served
as postmaster until 1913. A son of Russian
Jewish immigrants, Specter was born in
Chicago during the Civil War, but moved with
his family to East Chicago when the first iron
and steel mills were built there. His brother,
Issac, became a beer distributor based in the
wilds of what became the Calumet section,
and there he trained wild horses that pulled
his huge beer wagons. That experience with
spirited horses led Issac to become an early
member of the volunteer fire department,
which he headed in 1902 (one of Issac's jobs
being to slip the heavy harnesses onto the fire
horses whenever the fire whistle sounded).
Moses Specter was the father of Melvin
Specter, a long-time civic leader who for more
than sixty years has practiced law in East
Chicago. Photo from the Specter Collection

*Despite streets made mostly of sand, the
horseless carriage made an early appearance
in East Chicago. The gentleman in the derby
being chauffered about town may be a major
turn-of-the-century politico. At least, he seems
to be the same person who appears later in
the photo with Mayor DeBriae, Police Chief
Higgins, and East Chicago's finest. Photo
from the East Chicago Historical Society*

3

THE TWENTIETH CENTURY WONDER

The Lake Shore and Michigan Southern Railroad (New York Central) carried construction workers from South Chicago to Indiana Harbor in 1901 to build the town and the new mill of Inland Steel. For many years afterward, this and other railroads stopping in Indiana Harbor were the popular means of traveling to and from Chicago. By 1909, 125 trains a day stopped at Indiana Harbor. Photo from the East Chicago Historical Society

Magic

Indiana Harbor went up like a Hollywood set. Even as the harbor was being dug and the steel mill erected, the Lake Michigan Land Company leveled the sand ridges, laid out streets, installed sewers, hooked into the existing water, electric, and gas systems, built six hundred houses and stores, built the finest hotel south of Hyde Park, caused a school to be built, influenced the transportation service into and out of town, provided electric light and gas, paved a few macadam streets and cement sidewalks and put into place many miles of boardwalks, planted five thousand shade trees, reserved land for a lakefront public park and another park south of 141st Street, dedicated a strip of land for houses fronting the lake, and generally created and promoted a boom town.

Within three years, the new industrial city of Indiana Harbor, just nineteen miles southeast of downtown Chicago, was a reality, a phenomenon the land company called, "The Twentieth Century Wonder".

It was a real estate agent's paradise, and the place fairly swarmed with sellers and buyers. Lots half again as wide as Chicago lots (thirty-five and fifty feet wide instead of twenty-five) sold on easy terms for $225 and up. Agents attempted to demonstrate that small investors could ride an increase in prices into a handsome profit, and that large investors could get rich quick. To prove it, the land company provided free transportation from Chicago to Indiana Harbor, the center of what they promised would be the greatest manufacturing region in the United States.

In promoting the new town, real estate salesmen stressed that Indiana Harbor was no mere subdivision, but the fourth ward of the city of East Chicago, an incorporated city, having a mayor and board of aldermen. As a measure of the town's stability, the salesmen brought lists of those who backed Indiana Harbor: Albert DeWolfe Erskine, president of the East Chicago Company (into which previous land companies had merged); Honore Palmer, vice president; Potter Palmer, Jr., treasurer; Owen F. Aldis of the firm of Aldis, Aldis, Northcote & Company; John V. Farwell, Jr., of the J. V. Farwell Company; and Stanley McCormick, of the McCormick Harvester Works—all conservative and strong financially. The salesmen also stressed the quality of the townspeople and, in what turned out to be wanton irony, the town's clean air.

Transportation was a big draw. By 1904, 45 passenger trains stopped daily at Indiana Harbor, and the Lake Shore & Michigan Southern was building a fifteen thousand dollar passenger station on Regent Street, about three hundred feet north of Watling Street. A trolley, the South Shore, connected Indiana Harbor with East Chicago, and would soon be a feeder for an electric railway that was expected to run from Cleveland to Chicago and pass through Indiana Harbor. And if that was not enough, a passenger boat carrying five hundred people plied between Chicago and Indiana Harbor. For the industrialist or businessman, transportation was even more attractive. The railroads entering Indiana Harbor were the finest in the country, and railroad companies were investing a great deal of money in equipping themselves to handle the ever-increasing business of Indiana Harbor. Five trunk-line railroads passed through Indiana Harbor, and four belt lines connected all railroads outside the harbor. Without question, Indiana Harbor factories enjoyed unsurpassed freight facilities.

And through the building period in which physical assets appeared magically, people continuously filled the town beyond its capacity. First it was the construction workers, mostly commuting from Chicago. Then came the "move-ins" from surrounding towns, including South Chicago, to get in on the boom. Then workers transferred in by industries came, including management, skilled, and semi-skilled workers. And then there were the workers recruited from the fields of Europe and Asia. There was hardly a country in the world that didn't send people to Indiana Harbor, the ultimate melting pot. The developers fully expected that Indiana Harbor would be a city of ten thousand inhabitants by mid-1905.

To accommodate the initial influx, a tent city sprang up while others slept in box cars, shacks, other temporary dwellings, or wherever they could escape the ever-present sand fleas. The first man to sleep in his own bed was an innkeeper, Captain Friederich, who built the Harbor Hotel, the community's first. When he opened his doors to the public, however, he had nothing to offer but bare walls and bare floors. Because of the swamps and stumpy condition of the land between his hotel and the train station, the livery people had not figured out a way to deliver the four thousand dollars worth of furniture he had ordered. Nevertheless, the demand for sleeping space was so great that more than seventy-five guests paid for the privilege of sleeping on the floor.

Conditions of the tent city soon caused churches to arrive in the town. One day, the missionary spirit of Reverend Leazenby, the Methodist minister in East Chicago, prompted the pastor to hike over the treacherous ridgeland prairie and swamp east of East Chicago to investigate rumors of a city being born full-grown. When he finally arrived at the tent city he heard the unmistakable moaning of a woman. Stopping for a closer look, he lifted the flap of the tent to find one woman consoling another woman, who was holding and rocking a dead baby, and sobbing a pathetic apostrophe: "Why, oh why, God, did you lead us to this forsaken land?"

After Reverend Leazenby introduced himself, the grieving mother begged him for a Christian burial for her baby, and he agreed. In a short while, Methodists, Baptists, Lutherans, and Catholics joined with the Methodist pastor for the burial. That service started a chain of events that not only brought into being a Methodist church but established the basis for other churches. On October 12, 1901, Reverend Leazenby preached his first religious service, and, in a pointed allusion to the challenge of living in Indiana Harbor, took for his text a verse from St. John, "Ye are my friends if ye do whatsoever I command you."

By 1904, eight churches had organized and were holding services. In addition to the Methodist, there were a Baptist, Episcopal, Christian, German Evangelical, German Lutheran, and two Catholic churches. Houses had replaced tents, but because of certain building restrictions supply never caught up with demand. Many people who worked in Indiana Harbor had to live elsewhere, a practice that continues to the present. Hotel space had doubled—to the Harbor Hotel had been added the magnificent South Bay Hotel, which was built at the incredible turn-of-the-century cost of sixty-five thousand dollars.

Meanwhile, city services, under the administration of second-term East Chicago mayor William Hale, proved more than adequate. The pumping station continued to furnish Lake Michigan water to buildings in town. A complete sanitary sewer system—the Berlin system—seemed to assure a healthy condition. A sixteen thousand dollar schoolhouse, Lincoln School, on 136th Street between Elm and Fir, accommodated children of all nationalities, and responded to their specific needs. Citizens looked forward to a police and fire station on Watling Street, at the head of Pennsylvania Avenue. At the same time, community ammenities appeared. Two weekly newspapers ran successfully, and the Indiana Harbor Yacht Club, with a membership of almost three hundred, built a twenty-five hundred dollar clubhouse.

While Indiana Harbor was becoming a comprehensive and cosmopolitan community, Robert E. Tod and Henry C. Frick completed the immense outer harbor, the only deep-water harbor in Indiana. It seemed only a matter of time before it would open up a great lake traffic, and plans were made for the summer of 1904 to extensively build up the land along the harbor with warehouses, elevators, and docks. The inner harbor, too, after a gigantic 1903 Canal Day celebration in which Govorner Goodrich participated, was optimistically expected to be completed within two years, with seven miles of dockage and factories and elevators lining its banks.

Indeed, industry was already making its move. Inland Steel had spent almost two million dollars erecting and equipping its immense open-hearth steel mill, and in 1904 the company was enlarging its plant and expecting to employ more than twelve hundred men. Other factories along the canal route were just becoming operative, including plants of the Ward Dickey Steel Company, the Standard Forgings Company, and the American Steel foundries. Across the canal oppposite Inland, Henry Clay Frick sat on his three hundred acres, but it was widely understood that he would eventually erect not only a coke plant, but also a ten million dollar steel plant. On the east side of Indiana Harbor, just across the municipality line, the Illinois Steel Company of South Chicago was erecting a three million dollar plant to manufacture cement, a plant that would employ another six hundred people upon opening, and more than a thousand shortly thereafter.

Indiana Harbor was billed as "The Twentieth Century Wonder" in this 1904 brochure issued by the East Chicago Company. Notice the emphasis on living quality—the fine homes on Pennsylvania Avenue, the inset of the sailboat, and the relatively few smoke-stacks. Photo from Joseph Costanza

Albert De Wolfe Erskine founded Indiana Harbor by organizing the Lake Michigan Land Company, persuading the Block brothers to build a million dollar open-hearth mill, generally managing the building up of the town, and organizing its first bank, the Indiana Harbor State Bank. Sketch by Andrew J. Biancardi

Henry Clay Frick, the coke king, bought three hundred acres on the northwest side of the canal's main leg and helped pay for the digging of the canal. Although most people expected him to build a huge steel mill there, the land eventually passed to Princeton University, and then became the site of Mark Manufacturing Company and its successor companies. Sketch by Andrew J. Biancardi

Owen Franklin Aldis headed the Lake Michigan Land Company, which bought the land that is Indiana Harbor and built hundreds of houses and stores there on the original townsite. He is better known as the man who introduced skyscrapers to the world and who changed Chicago's skyline in the late nineteenth century. Sketch by Andrew J. Biancardi

Built entirely with private funds, the outer harbor was essentially finished the same year it was begun, 1901. Between a breakwater (north pier) that extended twelve hundred feet into Lake Michigan and a similar pier to the south, dredgers dug to a depth of twenty-one feet. When it was completed, the federal government took over the harbor and maintained it thereafter. Photo from the East Chicago Historical Society

The Indiana Harbor Ship Canal (nee Calumet Canal) became a reality when, in 1901, Henry Clay Frick and Robert Elliot Tod agreed to pay for 60 percent of its cost. Originally laid out and dug in 1888 as a giant ditch, the canal was deepened and widened to accommodate large lake vessels, thanks to the liberal application of mulepower. Photo from Inland Steel Company

As soon as the harbor had been dredged, Inland Steel began to use it as a receiving point for railroad ties. A spur track was run parallel to the dock on the south side and as sailboats and small steamers were unloaded, the ties were either stored on the sand or loaded on the cars and removed. The photo shown here of the first Inland dock is of a later date. From the Van Horne Collection

Even after huge lake ships began to arrive, fishermen continued to squat on the northwest side of the canal's main leg. Despite gargantuan industry and the heavy traffic of ore boats and tankers, the waters just off Indiana Harbor still attract some of the most sought-after fish in Lake Michigan. Photo from the East Chicago Historical Society

On July 21, 1902, a little more than one year after construction began, Inland Steel poured the first steel ingots to be formed in the Calumet Region of Indiana. This crew may have been part of that achievement. Photo from the Inland Steel Company

Governor Winfield T. Durbin dedicated the canal (inner harbor) amid much pomp and ceremony and cannon fire in October, 1903. More than three thousand people, including Chicago Mayor Carter Harrison II and future Vice President Charles W. Fairbanks, turned out for the ceremony on the lakefront. Two hundred feet wide and twenty-one feet deep, the canal when completed extended south- westerly a mile and a half, where it branched off in two directions, south and west. Not much work was accomplished on the canal, however, until 1907, shortly after Carl A. Westberg took charge of its development. As it was completed, the canal was turned over to the government in sections. Photo from Nassau & Thompson, Inc.

When fully operational, the outer harbor and inner harbor (canal) made Indiana Harbor the state's busiest port. An early visitor was the SS Vulcan, *shown here being unloaded by means of electrical lifting magnets, probably the first cargo of pig iron on the Great Lakes unloaded by this means. The first oil tanker arrived at Indiana Harbor on May 19, 1912, two years after Standard Oil built its docks on the west leg of the canal. Later, Sinclair and Socony Vacuum (Mobil) operated refineries on the canal, while Roxana (Shell) and Empire (Cities Service) refined oil a short distance from the canal, and piped gasoline to their docks on the canal for shipment. Photo from Inland Steel Company*

John R. Farovid, a Harvard graduate, was the first real estate salesman for the East Chicago Company in Indiana Harbor, and sold the first lot there. After spinning off into his own highly successful real estate business, Farovid in 1909 bought the Citizens State Bank and merged it with his real estate business to create the Citizens Trust and Savings Bank. Photo from the East Chicago Historical Society

Early Indiana Harbor real estate agents abounded in such great numbers that they resorted to almost anything to attract attention to their services. Even when the logic eluded observers, the promotion usually drew a crowd. Here, to the amusement of a variety of onlookers, a clown calls a pig that pulls a sled carrying Dorothy Gastel and Kathryn Schock through a snowy Indiana Harbor Street on behalf of the Gastel Agency. Photo from the Kathryn Schock Gale Collection

Captain Charles A. Friedrich built the first hotel in Indiana Harbor in 1901. Born in Germany, he sailed the seven seas in the Fatherland's merchant marine, before switching in 1869 to the heavily-trafficked Great Lakes, where he captained a variety of ships. After marrying in 1898, however, his days on the captain's deck were numbered, so he opened the Harbor Hotel and became a land-lubber. Cap Friederich soon became a familiar Indiana Harbor character who cheerfully regaled anyone who would listen with endless adventurous sea stories. Photo from the Encyclopedia of Genealogy and Biography of Lake County, Indiana

The South Bay Hotel was built in 1903 by Owen Franklin Aldis at the behest of Leopold Block. The finest hotel south of Hyde Park, it was created to accommodate the affluent mill superintendents, entrepreneurs, and important visitors. Designed in the grand manner of seaside resort hotels, the South Bay featured wide verandas, comfortable rooms, and large public areas, including an ample lobby, and ballroom, in which the fanciest dances of the community were held. Even after 1907 when Inland Steel began to build into Lake Michigan, as seen here, the hotel maintained its grandeur. Photo from the East Chicago Historical Society

Indiana Harbor, Ind.

East of the South Bay Hotel, across what became Lees Park, was a block of elegant mansions occupied by Indiana Harbor's elite. The one home that can be seen in this view was owned by John Stephens, a Muncieite and Inland Steel's first general superintendent. All management personnel were required to live within fifteen minutes of the plant's whistle, which sometimes invited their urgent attention. Prior to 1906, plant executives also favored nearby Baltimore Street and Commonwealth Avenue. Skilled and semi-skilled workers lived mainly on Block and Pennsylvania avenues. Photo from the East Chicago Historical Society

The last home on Aldis Avenue was owned by J. G. Danks, the Muncieite who laid out the original Inland Steel plant. Danks married a daughter of John Stephens. It would appear that at the time this photo was taken, Lake Michigan had taken a hungry bite out of the Danks residence. Photo from the Van Horne Collection

The main business section of the original Indiana Harbor townsite was anchored by the O'Brien Block, the three-story structure shown here, with stores on the first floor and apartments above. The O'Brien Block also held Indiana Harbor's first movie house, operated by Louis Greenfield, a man who went on to become a Hollywood mogul of the silent screen era. Photo from the Van Horne Collection

The East Chicago Company occupied the entire first floor of this large building on Pennsylvania Avenue across from the O'Brien Building. It was headquarters for an army of commission real estate salesmen who each morning commuted to Indiana Harbor from Chicago, and each evening returned home. Photo from the East Chicago Historical Society

Oscar Goerg (later Anglicized to George), Indiana Harbor's first pharmacist, began in the community as the junior partner of a Hammond man named Hodges. He operated the Harbor pharmacy, advantageously located between the East Chicago Company and a dry goods store. From 1906 to 1910, Goerg also served as city clerk. Photo from the Van Horne Collection

Bruno Schreiber, shown here with his wife and son, established the first plumbing business in town. He also operated a hall that was used by various organizations, including early churches. A member of the board of safety and leader of many other community organizations, Schreiber also helped found the Gennesareth Lutheran Church, which operated the only Protestant parochial school in the Twin City. Photo from the Van Horne Collection

Willard Van Horne, a pioneer Indiana Harbor lawyer, came to the community in September, 1902, two months after graduating from law school, and became one of the Harbor's most influential citizens. Not only did Van Horne build up an extensive and prestigious law practice, he became keenly active in political and civic affairs. He was elected a state representative for the first of several times in 1910. An avid joiner, Van Horne probably did more than anyone else to promote lodges in the Twin City. Photo from the East Chicago Chamber of Commerce

Suppliers of hardware, plumbing, electric wiring, and construction materials flourished, as six hundred buildings went up in Indiana Harbor during the town's first three years. Although the woman in the doorway is uni-dentified, she may be the wife of Otto C. F. Seehase, a Tolleston contractor who moved into town just as soon as ground was broken for the new harbor in 1901, and opened the first Indiana Harbor hardware store. Photo from the East Chicago Historical Society

Barker's Fair Store at 3415 Michigan Avenue, left, was Indiana Harbor's first store. Built in 1901, it was operating before Inland Steel was built and even before most of the pioneer familes arrived. The store carried house furnishings, notions, baby buggies, pots and pans, stoves, and anything else a resident of a frontier community could wish. A second store, right, sold furniture, and when Henry Barker introduced the town's first home delivery, bottom, most of the community turned out to witness the event. Photo from the East Chicago Chamber of Commerce

A cyclone hit Indiana Harbor in March, 1904, destroying or severely damaging much of the newly-built original townsite. One of the buildings leveled was the new brick store of Louis Barker, which trapped its owner in the rubble. When workers from Inland Steel arrived on the scene they attempted to rescue Barker, who was still alive and able to tell the workers to take their time. Alas, a worker sawed the wrong beam and the building collapsed on Barker, killing him. Photo from the East Chicago Historical Society

Mrs. Henry Barker and her daughter, Marian, and son pause here in their pony-drawn cart in front of the second Barker's Fair Store, rebuilt following the Cyclone of 1904. Photo from the collection of Marian Barker Janson

71

Although most streets were made of sand, at an early date, the East Chicago Company macadamized a few key streets, which encouraged the use of horse-drawn vehicles to travel about the new town. Photo from the Van Horne Collection

Members of the Cyclists' Club of early Indiana Harbor went where no other vehicles could, ranging in time to Chicago's Jackson Park, southern Lake County, and, via a roundabout route, to the Indiana Dunes Country. In winter, most cyclists became ice skaters, gliding as far as what became downtown Gary. Their chief obstacle, however, was the cement plant, which spewed dust sometimes a quarter-inch thick onto the frozen sloughs. Photo from the George Huish Collection

Baseball quickly became the popular team sport of Indiana Harbor, with teams using a field just outside the Inland Steel gate and another near the Auditorium. The first major team was the Harbor Indians. On a second level were teams such as the Nagdemans. Before long, Inland fielded its own team, shown here. Photo from Inland Steel Company

Young women from comparatively affluent families moved around sandy Indiana Harbor on their own steeds. Here Mary Walsh, displaying perfect sidesaddle form, explores 135th and Elm streets, early Indiana Harbor's great outback. Photo from Nassau & Thompson, Inc.

Steve Kish and two youngsters sailed to Michigan City in 1912 aboard the SS Theodore Roosevelt as part of the Inland Steel annual employee picnic. Inland began these outings in 1911, the year it formed the Inland Steamship Company. Children and their parents boarded a ship at the blast furnace dock in the morning, and were returned there in the evening. This mode of transportation was discontinued in 1915 after the SS Eastland, chartered by the Western Electric Company as an excursion boat for the company's annual picnic, overturned in the Chicago River, killing 812 people. Photo from the East Chicago Historical Society

Photographs by Buchstaber, Indiana Harbor's pioneer photographer, were in great demand by early Harborites. His shop on Pennsylvania Avenue (later on Guthrie) was frequently used as a backdrop for poses, such as this one by a family recording a momentous event, the acquisition of a horseless carriage. Photo from the East Chicago Historical Society

Vaudeville provided much of the commercial entertainment in pioneer Indiana Harbor. Here a troupe is shown at the Gem Theater, 3419 Michigan Avenue, one of several movie theaters owned and operated by Julius Nassau. Photo from Nassau & Thompson, Inc.

Julius Nassau and his wife Anna, shown in these two portraits, owned most of the movie theaters in Indiana Harbor, Whiting, and Gary until the Great Depression. At that point he joined his father, Charles, in the news distribution and office equipment and supplies business. When Charles died and his partner Harry G. Thompson retired, Julius took over the business, along with his aunt, Mary Pitzele. They subsequently passed the business on to David L. Nassau and O. S. Pitzele. Photos from Nassau & Thompson, Inc.

James A. Patterson arrived in Indiana Harbor in 1901 and succeeded as an attorney to such an extent that he was able to add offices in Gary and Hammond. As Indiana Harbor's most prominent attorney in the pre-World War I era, Patterson was elected prosecuting attorney for the Thirty-first Judicial Circuit in 1912. Like many others in Indiana Harbor, he was a native of Sharon, Pennsylvania. Photo from A Standard History of Lake County, Indiana, and the Calumet Region

Frank Callahan (left) and Monroe Schock, two bricklayers, came to Indiana Harbor in 1904 to exploit the building boom, and did. After forming a partnership, they specialized in brick buildings and erected some of the most important structures in the Harbor, including the O'Brien Block, the Commercial Club, the Methodist Church, the Christian Church, the Farovid Block, the Gillette Building, the Barker Block, the Auditorium, and numerous other business blocks, residences, and flat buildings. Monroe & Schock also started the Calumet Laundry, and they both participated in public affairs. In 1914, Callahan, a Democrat, became mayor running on the Citizens' ticket, and again in 1922, running on the Independent ticket. He refused to run for a third term because of what he termed the unenforceablity of the Prohibition laws. Meanwhile, Schock took over the laundry and operated it successfully for many years. Photo from the East Chicago Historical Society

Maude Mauger, whose father ran a teaming, express, and ice business just northeast of the Pennsy tracks, was briefly married to Jimmie Ward, the aerialist who once set an altitude record. This photo of them may have been taken at the 1911 International Aviation Meet held on Chicago's lakefront. One of a family of beautiful young women, Maude Mauger later married Sonny Sheetz, co-owner of the Big House in Indiana Harbor, the Chicago area's largest and most popular gambling casino. Photo from the Alice Perkins Wamshar Collection

Motive power for early dairies was housed as close to milk consumers as possible. The Alexander and McKimpson barns were located at 3517 Grapevine Street, right in the middle of one of Indiana Harbor's toniest blocks. Photo from the East Chicago Historical Society

Pete Giannini and Joe Esola, shown here, ran the pioneer Indiana Harbor Fruit Store, which apparently spawned other businesses. The Esola family ran a saloon at the Four Corners, and Giannini, in partnership with Joie Stallworth, ran the community's favorite ice cream shop, an automatic stopping place for early citizens out for a stroll. Photo from the East Chicago Historical Society

Indiana Harbor's earthy answer to the Tod Opera House was the Auditorium, shown here in this advertisement. It served a variety of functions, from mass meetings to boxing matches, and was a favorite watering hole of Harborites for half a century. Photo from the East Chicago Historical Society

The Auditorium Liquor House

B. & M. COHEN, Proprietors

TELEPHONE 552

The Auditorium

WILL RENT FOR BALLS, PARTIES, PUBLIC MEETINGS, THEATRE PERFORMANCES, ETC.
AND HAS A SEATING CAPACITY OF 800
KITCHEN IN CONNECTION
It Contains Lodge Hall and Fine Office Rooms with All Modern Conveniences

DON'T FORGET that the Auditorium Liquor House carries the largest and finest line of Liquors and Cigars in Lake County and retails at wholesale prices.

COR. 3436 MICHIGAN AVENUE AND GRAPVINE STREET

The Muncieites

The perfect boom town of Indiana Harbor began to change in 1904, however. To get Inland started, R.J. Beatty, a heavy investor who became Inland's first general manager as well as a board member, had brought in steel experts from Muncie, where Beatty had owned a steel mill of his own. Thus, he imported such Muncieites as J. G. Danks to lay out the Inland plant, John H. McGrath to design and superintend the open hearths, and John Stephens to serve as Inland's first general superintendent. To these and other key people, Beatty added hundreds of skilled and semi-skilled workers, many of them sheet men, whom he ran up to Indiana Harbor from Muncie during 1902 in special trains. These Muncieites lived in the American community adjacent to Inland Steel and formed the base population layer of Indiana Harbor. But their community roles were soon to change.

As members of the Amalgamated Association of Iron and Steel Workers, the blue collar Muncieites resisted attempts by Inland to void an agreement with the union limiting sheetmen's workweek to an agreed upon amount of production or forty hours of work, whichever came first. Presuming it had an economically vulnerable company on the ropes, the union threatened to strike. Needing full production from the entire plant to generate profit sufficient to survive, Inland threatened the sheet mill workers with lifetime blacklisting. Both sides carried out their threats.

In mid-1904, the sheet mill workers struck, and stayed out for nine months. Ironically, though, the union saved Inland from bankruptcy. Had Inland continued with the sheet mill's poor productivity, the company would have succumbed to fiscal anemia. At the end of the strike, the blacklisted Muncieites found all bridges behind them burned. There was no place to go and no place to stay, no job at Inland and no going back to Muncie. They solved that dilemma by finding jobs in real estate, insurance, banking, and non-steel plants, notably the Buffington cement plant, which although part of U.S. Steel seemed to operate independently. In a surprisingly short time, they worked their way into the power structure of the community. Thus, the blacklisted Muncieites became prominent in the social, economic, and political life of Indiana Harbor, and established a beachhead to which other Muncieites who had not been blacklisted gravitated.

The great and enduring irony of the blacklisting is that it put community power into the hands of people who would otherwise have had little or no power in the mill. Eventually, the original Muncieites, their offspring, other Muncieites they attracted, and others who shared Muncie *Middletown, U.S.A.* values pervaded every layer of Indiana Harbor society. Muncieites and like-minded people invested their energies in churches, schools, lodges, civic organizations, social service institutions, and all organizations benefiting the community, and became prominent in them. They also operated stores and small businesses, held political positions, and influenced political affairs. In short, for approximately fifty years, Muncieites ran the town.

John Stephens, Inland Steel's first general superintendent, was born in England of a family that for several generations had been in the iron and steel business. He emigrated to western Pennsylvania, where he became operational head of several iron and steel companies, then went to Muncie to head Midland Steel, and then to Indiana Harbor to start up Inland Steel. Several members of John Stephens' family became prominent in Indiana Harbor. Photo from Inland Steel Company

Sheet workers arrived from Muncie in 1902 with other skilled and semi-skilled workers to start the new Inland Steel mill. When the Muncie sheetmen struck the company at a time when Inland could hardly pay its bills, the company retaliated by blacklisting the workers for life, and replacing them with workers from Vandergrift, Pennsylvania. It is not known whether the group of early sheet workers shown here are Municieites or their Vandergrift replacements. Photo from Inland Steel Company

John W. Lees succeeded John Stephens as Inland's general superintendent. He and his wife also became a standard for prestige in the community, admired by children as well as adults. Each year, the Leeses put on a party for the children of Inland management, at which each was given a gold coin. They also gave parties for the children of the public schools, both in the schools and at the lakefront park named for him, and donated a huge pipe organ to the First Baptist Church of Indiana Harbor. Photo from Inland Steel Company

Police Chief Charles E. Bowen, shown here with Indiana Harbor's finest, was one of the many Muncie imports who left Inland to become community leaders. Bowen had arrived in Indiana Harbor in August, 1901, and worked as a soaking pit heater. In 1905, shortly after the Amalgamated strike at Inland, Bowen joined the Indiana Harbor police force, and when fellow Democrat Frank Callahan became mayor in 1914, Bowen became police chief. Photo from Nassau & Thompson, Inc.

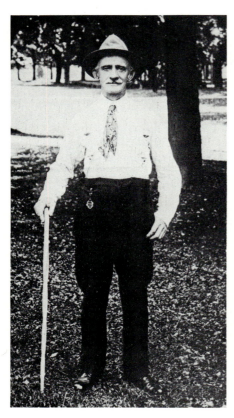

William Fox, a Welshman from Cleveland by way of Joliet, was brought in by Clevelander John Lees in 1903 to superintend Inland's bar mill, which began operation November 2, 1902, but had never performed as anticipated. With the help of still another Clevelander, Tom Campbell, a roll designer, Fox gradually improved the mill until it worked profitably. Photo from the John Fox Collection

George H. Huish, center, arrived in Indiana Harbor in 1902 on a special train from Muncie. After attending Twin City schools and serving in World War I, he became publisher of the Calumet News, at first a twice-weekly local newspaper, and commander of American Legion Post 266. He created the Distinguished Community Service Award, which William H. Kleppinger, left, presented to John W. Lees, right. Photo from the East Chicago Historical Society

Bert C. Lukens, a Muncieite who came to Indiana Harbor via South Bend, opened Central Drug Store in 1907 in partnership with Dr. C. C. Robinson and Dr. Frank E. Stephens. It became the community's informal "town hall," where the shakers and movers met daily for coffee, and other citizens stopped to gossip. It also was the South Shore trolley stop. The group of mostly barefoot children here seem to be on their way to some outing, perhaps an event at distant Washington Park, whose baseball field on Euclid Avenue the trolley ran past. Photo from the Van Horne Collection

Musical Chairs

Just as the Harbor's power structure began to change starting in 1904, its physical arrangement began to change in 1906. That was the year that the Baltimore and Ohio Railroad accommodated U.S. Steel and the new town of Gary by relocating its tracks several blocks south of the lakeshore as it passed through Gary. The B & O accomplished this by bending its trunk line in a northwest-southeast direction from the head of Michigan Avenue in Indiana Harbor to the Gary border. Instead of running hard by Lake Michigan, the tracks angled through the town's finest residential neighborhood, altering the looks and the character of The Twentieth Century Wonder forever. Until 1906, that part of the original townsite nearest Lake Michigan had many of the characteristics of a seashore resort. It had the luxurious South Bay Hotel, a fine beach, a yacht club and special breakwater for private boats, as well as large homes on or near the shoreline, with platted space for hundreds of others. Foreign-born mill recruits lived some distance away over sandy wastes along Cedar Street (now Main Street) and flanking streets, in what was popularly referred to as Hunkeytown. Industry was neatly stretched along the canal and belt line so as not to impinge significantly on the residential area. That pattern changed with the bending of the B & O, as affected homes were simply lifted from their foundations, placed on huge flatbeds with wheels, and rolled to other parts of the community, mostly to Grapevine and Fir streets, and to the distant Park Addition.

As a *coup de grace,* the state of Indiana, at the same time, passed a made-land bill that allowed property owners to build into Lake Michigan. This bill motivated Inland Steel to immediately begin to acquire lake property adjacent to the mill, where the new line of the B & O cut its Sherman-like swathe through the original townsite. Less than a decade later, when World War I broke out in Europe and the war-induced demand for steel required Inland to expand greatly, the company completed its land acquisitions in the lakeside community, and began to build a second plant, right on the lake and eventually into it. As a result, many of the remaining lake district homes were moved, the eastern part of the neighborhood nearest the lake was never developed, the magnificent South Bay Hotel was razed, and the day of the resort colony ended.

As the big houses of community leaders rolled westward over the Pennsy tracks and southward toward the Park Addition, other people on streets near the lakeshore followed in the trail. The so-called American community tended to resettle and stretch from a baseline of Michigan Avenue southward along Grapevine, Fir, and even Hemlock streets. Meanwhile, the easily-assimilated Swedes of Standard Forgings began to stretch southward from 137th Street along Ivy Street. Thus, three consecutive north-south streets (Fir, Grapevine, and Hemlock) formed a solidly native American and northern European corridor through Indiana Harbor that connected with the all American Park Addition, while two streets west, Swedish Ivy Street also connected with the Park Addition. As new Americans and northern Europeans who melded easily into the Muncie value system arrived in the community, they tended to settle in the American Corridor, on Ivy, or in the Park Addition, a six-block wide community of native whites and northern Europeans.

While this relocation process was going on, Romanians who had settled on Elm Street "backdoored" the erstwhile American community, flowing into Block Avenue and other remaining lake community streets from 135th Street northward. Soon thereafter, other immigrants who had settled in Hunkeytown followed suit. Before long, immigrants from eastern and southern Europe dominated the former American community. When rural blacks arrived from the South during World War I, those who worked at Inland Steel or the cement plant settled in the southernmost parts of such streets as Block and Pennsylvania, and in what remained of Hunkeytown. And when the Mexicans arrived as strikebreakers after the war, they settled right next to Inland Steel on the northernmost part of the lake community, the blacks and Mexicans forming bookends for what became an essentially immigrant, other-side-of-the-tracks section of town. Thus, in less than two decades, the most prestigious community in town, and perhaps in the Calumet Region, became if not a slum, at least the roughest part of town.

At the same time, a pattern of settlement that would last a half century was forming. Blacks who came to Indiana Harbor in a flow that waxed and waned from World War I onward settled in the south end of the original lakeshore community. They settled also on Carey and Drummond north of 141st Street, and in great numbers in the isolated New Addition, which was separated from the rest of Indiana Harbor by the then-unbridged Chicago, Indiana and Southern Railroad yards. Some blacks also settled near and on the property of Grasselli Chemicals in a neighborhood called Mush Rush, or Mud Rush, next to a neighborhood that was half Hungarian, a fourth Croatian, and a fourth Polish. Meanwhile, just prior to World War I, eastern European immigrants, out of space on their traditional streets, spilled over onto streets east of Grapevine and south of 137th Street. When World War I and the immigration laws of 1921 and 1924 practically stopped the flow of unskilled labor from Europe, the distribution pattern in Indiana Harbor became frozen. Immigrants already in the Harbor, their positions in the mill improved by seniority and training, dug in, especially securing the neighborhoods around their churches.

Until well after World War II, the result of the redistribution process begun in 1906 was a tightly confined Indiana Harbor community of European immigrants, having two islands of mill supervisory personnel (Marktown and Sunnyside), growing pockets of blacks and Mexicans, and strong fibers of native white Americans and Northern Europeans running north and south through it. Thus, there was very little mixing of these discrete ethnic parts of the world's ultimate mixing bowl. Even after various nationalities established churches south of the original townsite limits around which enclaves developed, foreign-speaking residents generally avoided the American corridor, except to pass through it, as well as avoiding black and Mexican neighborhoods. The mixing took place mainly at work for the men, in the schools for the children, and hardly at all for the women, and the fusion of the peoples of a hundred lands occurred almost imperceptibly.

Following the Baltimore and Ohio Railroad's relocation of its tracks in 1906, many of the homes in the resort-like lakeshore community were placed on flatbeds, as in this photo, and rolled to locations south of Michigan Avenue. Most of the homes were moved by Frank Orth, a Canadian bricklayer who arrived in the Harbor in 1903, erected many of the town's first brick buildings, and operated a brick factory in the dune country. The Van Horne home seen here was moved first from Regent Street to what remained of Commonwealth Avenue in 1907. Willard Van Horne, Jr., son of a pioneer Indiana Harbor attorney, is one of the small boys sitting on the porch. Photo from the Van Horne Collection

One of the first houses on fashionable Grapevine Street was this one at 3506. It was the residence of John P. Anderson. Shown in this 1902 photo were Mrs. Anderson and three sons, Walter, William, and Arthur, along with an out-of-town relative and an unidentified baby. Grapevine Street became the central north-south fibre settled by people displaced from the so-called American community close to the lake. Photo from the East Chicago Historical Society

Before the displaced Baptists built their first church at 3511-13 Fir Street in 1909, they met in the homes of William Huish and William Reese on Pennslyvania Avenue and in other homes and halls of the lakeside community. During that time, Halley Farr Waggener, a University of Chicago divinity student, commuted back and forth by rail from the campus to conduct services. Upon graduation, he became the church's first full-time minister. Here the Reverend and Mrs. Waggener are shown when they first came to the Harbor in 1902, and in 1952 when they returned for the church's fiftieth anniversary celebration. Photo from the East Chicago Historical Society

Early Park Addition homes were built southward from 141st Street (Columbus Drive) along Drummond and Carey streets. This pioneer home in the 141st block of Carey still stands. Notice that residents had to walk a gangplank to enter their home. Photo from the East Chicago Historical Society

Workers at the virtually all-Swedish Standard Forgings plant, known popularly as the Swedish penetentiary, settled mainly on Ivy Street, near the plant. Because of their close connection with the Swedish community in Chicago, Ivy Street Swedes frequently held gatherings and reunions, such as this one, with relatives and friends from old neighborhoods. Early Indiana Harbor Swedish families included Aldrin, Erickson, Johnson, Carlson, Kjellstrom, Nordberg, Forsberg, Soderstrom, Berg, Tolf, Larson, Lindberg, Nordquist, Oberge, Stromquist, Bergmark, Hokanson, and Nyquist. Photo from the Vern Aldrin Collection

What was derisively known as Hunkeytown centered around Cedar Street, shown here in the teens. Its main developer was Wolf Markovich, a Romanian Jew who came to Indiana Harbor in 1904 upon hearing that Inland Steel planned to import hundreds of workers from Romania. He built a saloon, boarding house, informal bank, and steamship agency on Cedar, and became a major real estate operator. At one point, Markovich's real estate holdings were so extensive that he paid more taxes than any entity in Indiana Harbor except Inland Steel. The residuum of the Markovich empire today is the March Travel Agency, still located on Main (nee Cedar) Street. Photo from the East Chicago Historical Society

85

Early 1900's
Romania Mica & *Transylvania Hall*
Corner of Pennsylvania ...

Transylvania Hall came into existence on Pennsylvania Avenue at Washington when Romanians replaced residents of the original lakeside community. It was one of many ethnic social centers. By 1920, when this photo was taken in front of Transylvania Hall, more than eight hundred Romanians lived in the Twin City, most of them in Indiana Harbor. That number increased by 50 percent during the twenties after World War I and prior to the Immigration Acts of 1921 and 1924, but also after that because Romanian immigrants were joining their families already established in Indiana Harbor. By 1930, one out of every ten foreign-born residents of the Twin City was Romanian. Photo from the East Chicago Historical Society

Guthrie Street, shown here, angularly connected the main commercial street of the American community (Michigan Avenue) with the main commercial street of foreign-born residents (Cedar Street), and was often the first street in Indiana Harbor new immigrants saw. Many newcomers arrived at the station of the Pennsylvania Railroad, right, tied together with a rope so they would not wander away. The theater at the left in the same building as the post office was aptly named the Liberty. Guthrie was the basing line for streets stretching southward settled mainly by foreign-born residents of Indiana Harbor, while Michigan was the main basing line for streets settled mainly by native Americans and Old Immigration arrivals. Photo from the East Chicago Historical Society

Esola's Tavern at the Four Corners, where the road leading to the "Old World" crossed the main artery of the "New World," was a popular watering hole of early real estate dealers and others involved in the Harbor's commercial life. Since many commissioned salesmen who lived in Chicago commuted daily to and from the Harbor, they often stopped at Esola's to catch up on the latest business gossip. Photo from the East Chicago Historical Society

The Gadzala family are shown here in front of their modest workman's cottage in Hunkeytown about 1906. Photo from the East Chicago Historical Society

Madame Antoinette Sherpetosky represented one of the leading examples of normative cultural fare in Indiana Harbor. A ballet dancer of considerable talent, she operated a studio in the neighborhood of the saloon at 3480 Guthrie which her parents, Stephen and Bessie, ran in the aughts. In the twenties, when entertainers displayed their talents from a band shell in Washington Park, Madame Sherpetosky's troupe invariably tripped fantastically and lightly as part of the programs. The Sherpetoskys were among the first eastern Europeans to settle in Indiana Harbor, when Joseph Sherpetosky, a Lithuanian, bought the third vacant lot on Guthrie, sold in 1901. Photo from the East Chicago Historical Society

Lithuanians organized into a parish in 1913, and soon built St. Francis of Assisi Roman Catholic Church at 3901 Fir Street. It was one of several churches that sprang up in a new neighborhood of foreign-born, south of the original townsite boundary on 137th Street, and west of Cedar. Other churches to locate in this neighborhood included Assumption of the Blessed Virgin Mary (Slovak) at 4002 Elm, Holy Ghost Greek Rite Catholic at 3719 Elm Street (Carpatho-Russian or Ruthenian), Holy Trinity (Slovak) at 3719 Elm Street, and St. George Serbian Orthodox at 4015 Elm Street. In this photo, the St. Francis congregation assembled for the traditional funeral photograph, in this case the funeral of a baby. The small boy in black to the right of the casket is Theodore Mason, Sr., who later became prominent in public affairs. Photo from the Mason collection

LINCOLN SCHOOL — INDIANA HARBOR, IND.

Lincoln School, built in 1903 between Elm and Fir on 136th Street, was at first the remotely-located school of the American community, but quickly became the great mixing bowl of Indiana Harbor, through which all children in the community, except those in the Park Addition, passed. Lincoln succeeded four rented rooms in the Pekonic Building on Watling Street, which comprised seven grades and emphasized manual training. On opening day, Lincoln admitted more than 336 and added 40 more pupils by squeezing chairs into the rooms. This was almost triple the enrollment of the preceding year in the Watling Street school. Counting kindergarten, enrollment at Lincoln was 426. Still, some pupils had to be turned away. To relieve the crowded conditions at Lincoln School, the first (of three) Eugene Field School was built on Commonwealth Avenue at Washington Street in 1904, a four-room, four-grade school that accommodated children who lived east of the Pennsy tracks. That same year, a Park Addition school capable of accommodating 100 pupils was established. Within four years, the population of Indiana Harbor flip-flopped from being practically all native born to being predominantly (85 percent) foreign-born. This meant that Lincoln School processed mainly children whose first language was not English. Photo from the East Chicago Historical Society

E. J. "Jimmie" Block is the least-known of the Block brothers, mainly because he was closer in age to the sons of Philip and Leopold than to his brothers. From the aughts until his death in 1939, E. J. worked in purchasing, ultimately becoming vice president of that function. An avid baseball enthusiast, E. J. played infield for several teams in Indiana Harbor, and to honor his memory the company donated to the citizens of the Twin City the E. J. Block Athletic Field. Ironically, at the dedication of what came to be known as Block Stadium on Memorial Day, 1942, and at an inspection tour of the company's new defense plant the same day, E. J.'s brother Philip over-exerted himself, which led to his death a month later, June 30, 1942.

4

ONE CITY

Mayor Edward DeBriae, shown here, center front, with the modest Twin City police force of the mid-aughts, became East Chicago's first Democratic mayor in 1906. Born in Buffalo, DeBriae and his partner, C. E. Hungerford, located in East Chicago in 1890, bought a lot, erected a building, and started a bakery, confectionery, and ice cream business that was hugely successful. Although he took over a city burdened with inherited debt, he nevertheless managed to install many needed internal improvements. During a 1907 strike at the Republic and Interstate rolling mills, in which laborers making fifteen cents an hour demanded a two cent raise, he and Chief Higgins, left front, assembled the strikers in front of City Hall and, with the aid of several interpreters, addressed them. In a settlement, the companies raised the hourly rate to 16.5 cents. From the East Chicago Historical Society

The Trappings

Although East Chicago and Indiana Harbor functioned as if they were separate cities, they gradually became unified in the essentials of operating a successful municipality. This process began with the educational system and the arrival of Edwin Nelson Canine, who became principal of East Chicago High School in 1904, and then superintendent of schools in 1905. He held that position for some two decades.

Canine put in place a unique educational system that, over time, gave residents a basis for trying to work and live together. Thoroughly pragmatic, Canine's system took into account both the English illiteracy of the foreign-born students and the reality that most male pupils would spend their careers in the mills. Among his many innovations, Canine individualized education with coach teachers, matched pupils with jobs in the community, tailored school work to pupils' ability, reduced subjects to a few crucial ones in what later educators would call a core program, kept the schools open in the summer, and introduced the first night school in Lake County with special classes for the foreign-born, including adults.

During the time that Canine was putting in place his revolutionary school system, the Twin City was growing faster than it ever had or ever would. From 1900 to 1910, Twin City population almost quintupled. This created a demand for ever more services, and kept the municipality in a constant state of impoverishment for which there seemed no relief. As the hordes of Europeans kept coming, each train full of immigrants disgorging new residents with needs of their own, the Twin City's infrastructure groaned under the added load. Fortunately, the new mayor elected in 1906, Edward DeBriae, practiced a variant of voodoo financing. Without visible means of financial support, DeBriae and his administration somehow managed to macadamize and pave miles of walks, lay many streets in brick, install vitrified and brick sewers, open two ten acre parks, build police stations in both East Chicago and Indiana Harbor, and erect a fine city hall.

These internal improvements resulted in part from revenues generated by the growth of the Calumet section, immediately south of Indiana Harbor. When Charles W. Hotchkiss opened the Indiana Harbor Belt in 1906, and Carl A. Westberg extended the canal's south leg two miles from the fork, industries came to Calumet in bunches. On the other hand, this rapid growth was an embarrassment of riches. More industry meant more people and both required still more services and space. With acquisitive Gary having extended its corporate limits to the Indiana Harbor border, and with the air rife with talk about amalgamating the Calumet Region's four principal cities in Indiana, the Twin City understandably began to display growing-pain twitches.

Finally, worry about too few services in too little space erupted on March 21, 1910, a moment that lives in infamy as "Gobble Day." Suffering by then from an acute attack of claustrophobia, the Twin City found relief in a preemptive strike against neighboring Hammond, which the Twin City whimsically annexed. In defense, startled Hammond laid itself on the mercy of archenemy Gary, which a week later annexed the Twin City, including Hammond, and for good measure Whiting. What resulted was an unprecedented political free-for-all that stopped just short of border war. Finally, the mayors of the various cities met at the summit and called the whole thing off, and on December 20, a Superior Court judge made it official. But Gobble Day resulted in a changed municipality. However momentarily, the Twin City had become a large city, and so it staffed up accordingly. It never completely retrenched. Overnight, the police department increased from eight to forty, as Mayor Schlieker proved to be even more of a fiscal sorcerer than DeBriae.

Gobble Day, however, was only the overture to a melodrama revolving around the growth of Calumet. Having heard that Baldwin Locomotive might build a western plant, Charles W. Hotchkiss, who by then had started a bank in Calumet, traveled to Philadelphia, set up an office, ran couriers back and forth to the Twin City, called in all the credits he had, and generally laid Baldwin under seige. He won. Baldwin bought 375 acres in his Calumet-Kennedy Land Company subdivision, and announced it would build a plant that would eventually employ fifteen thousand. What followed was the greatest scramble for land since the opening of the Indian territory. All loose lots in the Twin City were scarfed up, and the new Philadelphia Land and Improvement Company, whose president was City Judge Walter J. Riley, and whose stockholders were executives of Baldwin Locomotive, bought all unplatted land in Indiana Harbor. Alas, Baldwin did not build, most land buyers lost their investments, and the Philadelphia Land and Improvement Company sat on the Indiana Harbor property for years.

Mayor DeBriae's administration created a paid fire department, with Ben Flack as chief, and immediately equipped the East Chicago fire station next to the City Hall with a steam kettle, hose cart, and chief's buggy. The almost inaccessible Indiana Harbor station received a hose cart. In 1912, the Schlieker administration added a motor-driven pumper to the Indiana Harbor station, and another to the East Chicago station in 1913. The administration also equipped East Chicago with a hook and ladder in 1914, making the Twin City one of the first municipalities to have a motorized department. Here the leadership of the Indiana Harbor station is shown in 1911. Photo from the East Chicago Historical Society

Edwin N. Canine became superintendent of schools in 1905 and quickly installed a revolutionary educational system that took into account the almost total industrial environment of the city, as well as its more than three-quarters foreign-born population. Photo from the East Chicago Historical Society

Control of the city's water supply changed in 1907 when the Indiana Trust Company of Indianapolis, trustee since 1903 of the bankrupt Twin City water department, sold it to a private firm. The East Chicago-Indiana Harbor Water Company operated it until the city bought it back in 1924. However, the city did not gain complete control of its water until 1964 when the bonds were paid. For forty years, a portion of all revenue collected for water was set aside to pay off the bonds. Shown here are water plant workers of an early era. Photo from Nassau & Thompson, Inc.

The size of the Twin City's police force quintupled during the excitement of Gobble Day in 1910, when East Chicago annexed Hammond. After that action was nullified by consent among the cities involved, the inflated police force shrank to a more rational size, although still double what it had been before 1910. It is shown here in 1911, at a time when Leo McCormack, center front, was chief. Captain Michael Gorman, second from right, had the longest service on the force, joining it in 1898. McCormack, a former worker at Emlyn Steel, became chief on May 16, 1911, and mayor in 1918. Photo from the East Chicago Historical Society

A. G. Schlieker, M.D. became mayor in 1910, brought organization and management to city government, and invested heavily in improvements. During Schlieker's administration, a time when many new mills came to East Chicago, the city acquired the finest fire-fighting equipment in the state, invested in protecting riparian rights, improved parks, laid twenty miles of sidewalk, installed an ornamental street lighting system, constructed city docks and garbage incinerators, bought new police patrols, installed street signs, rebuilt sewers, built a municipal bath house, constructed new bridges, and constructed a new City Hall. Schlieker and another physician who became mayor, Raleigh P. Hale, married a pair of sisters named Phillips. From the Stuart Thomson Studios

The paddy wagon that became part of the expanded police department during the Schlieker administration demanded much less of patrolmen than the previous method. When Michael Gorman, a captain in the teens, joined the force in 1898, it took a great deal of strength to be a policeman. In a city not blessed with sidewalks nor even a horse-drawn police wagon, Gorman transported law breakers through the sand in a wheelbarrow to the two foot by four foot jail. Photo from the East Chicago Historical Society

Municipal services were supplemented by the voluntary efforts of the Boy Scouts, who organized in 1911. Scouts became especially active in clean-up campaigns and similar civic-improvement projects that required willing hands. During World War II they collected tons of much needed scrap during salvage drives and even served as messengers for the Office of Civilian Defense. The first troops were organized between 1911 and 1919 by Fred Woodbury, Walter Cox, C. C. Hahn, Reverend W. W. Bay, H. E. Shephard, and Herman W. Dickes, shown here at a dunes scout camp riding a motorcyle of the day. Photo from the East Chicago Historical Society

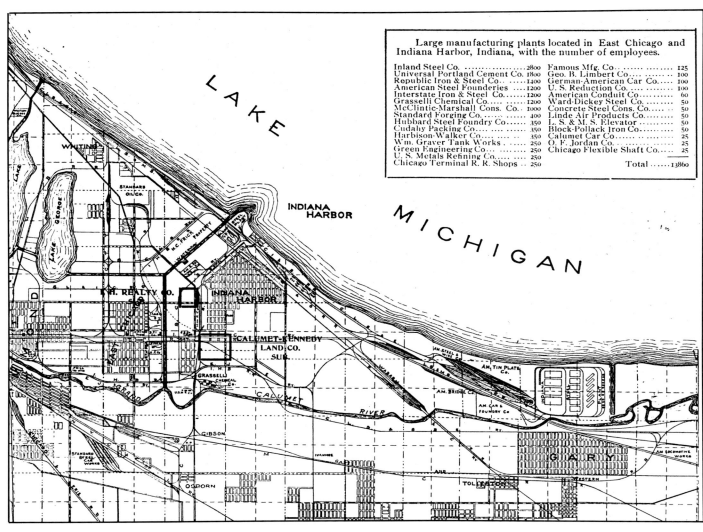

Inland Steel Co.	2800	Famous Mfg. Co.	125
Universal Portland Cement Co.	1800	Geo. B. Limbert Co.	100
Republic Iron & Steel Co.	1400	German-American Car Co.	100
American Steel Founderies	1200	U. S. Reduction Co.	100
Interstate Iron & Steel Co.	1200	American Conduit Co.	60
Grasselli Chemical Co.	1200	Ward-Dickey Steel Co.	50
McClintic-Marshall Cons. Co.	1000	Concrete Steel Cons. Co.	50
Standard Forging Co.	400	Linde Air Products Co.	50
Hubbard Steel Foundry Co.	350	L. S. & M. S. Elevator	50
Cudahy Packing Co.	350	Block-Pollack Iron Co.	50
Harbison-Walker Co.	350	Calumet Car Co.	25
Wm. Graver Tank Works	250	O. F. Jordan Co.	25
Green Engineering Co.	250	Chicago Flexible Shaft Co.	25
U. S. Metals Refining Co.	250		
Chicago Terminal R. R. Shops	250	Total	13860

The Calumet-Kennedy Land Company's subdivision, now called Calumet, is shown here south of Indiana Harbor proper and east of East Chicago.

*Albert C. Westberg, right, who joined the East Chicago Company in 1905, supervised the building of the canal, which was essentially complete by 1910. This set the stage on the south leg for development of metals refineries and other industries, and on the west leg for a concentration of oil refineries and docks.
Photo from the Janet Westberg Collection*

Colonel Walter J. Riley worked closely with Charles W. Hotchkiss in the development of the Indiana Harbor Belt Railroad, which complemented the Indiana Harbor Ship Canal. He also served as president of the Calumet Trust and Savings Bank and president of the Philadelphia Land and Development Company, which in 1912 bought all of the unplatted land in Indiana Harbor. Photo from the East Chicago Historical Society

The vast Baldwin site was known as "The Red Fence" because for seventeen years it was closed off literally by a red fence and, according to denizens who know local folk tales, occupied only by evil. It was not until 1929 when Empire Oil built a refinery on the Baldwin tract that the red fence came down and people lost their inhibitions about traversing the land. Shown here is a surveyor contemplating the land while the refinery is being built. Photo from the East Chicago Chamber of Commerce

Because of a fatal accident to a child whose mother was at work, Colonel Riley in 1913 created the St. Joseph's Home where nuns of the Carmalite Order cared for children whose mothers were at work. When the home's door-step became a drop for abandoned babies, however, the home quickly became an orphanage, eventually just for girls. Although operated by a Catholic order, the home was not restricted to Catholic children. During the day, the girls attended schools of the city, most of them at a nearby parochial grade school. Older girls usually attended Bishop Noll (nee Catholic Central) High School. Girls of the Carmalite Home in 1926 are seen here in Riley Park. Photo from the East Chicago Chamber of Commerce

Residents of Calumet stopped just short of conferring sainthood on Carrie Gosch, but did manage to have a school named for her. A teacher in the Twin City for more than a half century, she not only attended to the educational needs of generations of young people in the remote and unimproved Oklahoma (Calumet) section, but to their health, economic, and emotional needs as well. She is seen here as a young woman in 1900 with a group of students at the Berry Lake School. Photo from the East Chicago Historical Society

Growing Up in a Hurry

Before the Baldwin affair could be sorted out, however, the Great War started in Europe, and the Twin City turned its attention to supplying the combatants with the materials of war. At the same time, a new local tension appeared, one punctuated by patriotic gestures and altercations, as the largely foreign-born population of the Twin City took sides. On one side, the five hundred or so German-born citizens sympathized with the Fatherland and opposed shipping war materials to opponents of Germany. For their luckless chauvinism, they received undisguised abuse from the numerically greater Slavic population, the Slavs generally treating the Germans as spies and saboteurs. Thus, names changed. Not only did Schmidt become Smith but the German American Company became the General American Company. On the other hand, the Twin City's Hungarians denounced the bad press given to the Central Powers and swore full support to the Old Country. And when America joined the war in 1917, Serbians by the score returned to Europe to fight directly for their native land.

As U.S. entry into the war became increasingly likely, Allen P. Twyman, later a city judge, and Claude Dreesen organized a Twin City military company. On April 27, 1917, Company L was mustered into the Indiana National Guard, and the Twin City actually and symbolically marched off to war. After staying together for awhile, fifteen members of Company L were transferred to the Rainbow Division, the first division of U.S. soldiers to land in France, with others going to different units. Eighty-seven stayed together and served in France in 1918. Throughout the war, Twin City draftees filled out Company L to its full strength, as well as other units. Of these and other Twin City men who served, twenty-four died in battle. By Armistice Day, the Twin City had contributed a larger percentage of its young men to the war than any other city its size in the nation.

For all the tragedy that it generated, World War I occurred at a most advantageous time for the Twin City. Much of the community's industry had been put into place during the years just preceding the war, and the Twin City collectively was a ready-made defense plant. All that was required was conversion to wartime production. That was accomplished quickly and efficiently, as the self-described "Workshop of the Nation" became the self-described "Arsenal of the Nation," producing naval and military shells, heavy artillery, shrapnel casing, benzol, military acids, fabricated boats, submarine parts, naval and aircraft oils and fuels, and other ordnance equipment. The effect of the conversion was to accelerate the maturity of the Twin City.

Coordination of wartime industrial activities fell largely to Walter J. Riley, who had been instrumental in attracting much industry to the Twin City. Just prior to the outbreak of hostilities, Governor Goodrich had named Riley a member of the war governor's military staff, with the rank of colonel in the Indiana National Guard. Riley, who also had founded, in 1915, the Twin City's Manufacturers' Association, functioned as contact officer between the federal government and industry in converting local plants to munitions production. All communication between the local war industry and the War, Navy, Justice, and Treasury departments flowed through Riley. In all, he coordinated the production of more than twenty-five thousand men turning out the stuff of war. Simultaneously, and also working mainly with manufacturers, Riley headed the Twin City Liberty Loan campaigns, which were the first over-subscribed campaigns in the nation.

Thus, the war was a glorious moment for East Chicago and Indiana Harbor. In breaking all known production records and becoming a national arsenal, the Twin City achieved its majority, ready to go on with its adult life. The extent to which World War I accelerated the Twin City's development can be roughly seen in the rapid growth of its population. From 19,098 in 1910, it almost doubled to 35,967 in 1920, a direct result of industrial expansion to meet the wartime needs. Not only did Twin City plants fill out in the amount and kind of equipment, but also in sheer size. Perhaps the most dramatic expansion occurred at Inland Steel, which more than doubled in size.

With America's 1917 entry into the Great War, 125 Twin City men immediately volunteered for the army and petitioned to form themselves into their own company. They became Company L of the 151st Infantry, 38th Division—Allen P. Twyman captain, and Claude Dreesen first lieutenant. Their names are listed in this memorial in the Indiana Room of the Twin City's main library. Photo from the East Chicago Historical Society

Both East Chicago and Indiana Harbor applied for Red Cross charters in 1917, and as a visible symbol of their dedication and focus, volunteers in the Harbor built the hut shown here in a single day. It was used by women to collect and make medical supplies for the troops. Located on Fir Street near Michigan Avenue, the hut was demolished after the war. Also after the war, the two Red Cross groups melded into a single chapter. Photo from the East Chicago Historical Society

To spur workers on to new production records, servicemen often visited plants and made speeches. Here, a sailor named Blake exhorts Inland Steel workers to give their all for the war effort. Photo from the East Chicago Historical Society

The Twin City was the first municipality in the nation to exceed its Liberty Bond quota and it did it more than once. The effort was coordinated by Colonel Riley, ably assisted by block captains and lieutenants such as those shown here at Louis Saric's real estate office. Among those in this photo are Mrs. John W. Lees, wife of Inland Steel's general superintendent, and Beulah Hock Collins. Photo from the Kathryn Schock Gale Collection

The Troubles

This sudden blossoming during the war, however, did not prepare the community for events following the war. First came strife, then economic recession, then the tourniquets of immigration laws, then responses to Prohibition that technically transformed the hard-working citizenry of the Twin City into a camp of criminals, and finally economic apoplexy from which the Twin City recovered in a much-altered state.

Following World War I, labor trouble wracked the Twin City as never before. Agitators were everywhere, and industry looked for Reds in every shadow of the Twin City's mills. Meanwhile, the Twin City resounded with propaganda, threats, strikes, and an occasional bomb. Reds held numerous meetings and generated a torrent of propaganda that climaxed in May, 1919, with a parade through Twin City streets. Marchers waved red flags, flaunted revolutionary signs, and shouted chants for world revolution. When the Amalgamated union struck Inland Steel on September 22, 1919, Inland continued operating, but during the union shutdown, a serious explosion occurred in the gas washer and dryer for the number two blast furnace. When strikers barred entry to the plant, the company set up in-plant living facilities for non-strikers, foremen, and strikebreakers, many of whom were blacks imported from the rural South and Mexicans imported from the Southwest and Mexico. Those who moved in and out of the plant did so, however, without benefit of police protection, Mayor Leo McCormack being an ardent unionist.

Inevitably, scuffling escalated into a riot and when, on October 4, a strikebreaker shot at a picket, a menacing crowd of two thousand gathered at the Inland gate, threatening to storm it. With the situation now out of control, Mayor McCormack asked the governor to send in the militia, and the next day, Sunday, the entire state militia moved into Indiana Harbor. Five hundred militiamen positioned themselves at the gate to assure workers safe passage through the strikers. At the same time, the militia dried up Indiana Harbor to cut off the strikers' source of quick courage. Meanwhile, trouble broke out in Gary and the militia moved from Indiana Harbor to join police and sheriff forces there in a vain attempt to preserve order. At that point, October 6, the governor declared martial law not only for Indiana Harbor but Gary, and appealed to the U.S. Army to take over. Almost immediately, twenty-two hundred "regulars" materialized, and the mills began to operate, although it was not until early 1920 that the regular army moved out.

The strike changed the community in the long-term mainly by mixing into the population large numbers of blacks and Mexicans, two groups that did not meld readily with the entrenched residents. The blacks arrived first, at a time when the demand for labor increased dramatically following the economic blahs of 1914 and the onset of war in Europe. Mexicans came into Indiana Harbor right after the war and created there the densest concentration of Mexicans in the United States. Apart from racial and cultural stigmas, blacks and Mexicans attracted hostility from the eastern and southern European immigrants because they helped to frustrate the hopes of the Europeans. As much as the militia and the Army, the blacks and Mexicans had broken the strike, so long after the reason for the antipathy had been

blurred by time, blacks and Mexicans were lightning rods for antagonism, as anger toward their strikebreaking activities became generalized. It didn't matter that they had come not as hostile mercenaries. Gradually, but very gradually in a process that is not yet complete, the blacks and Mexicans, supplemented by Puerto Ricans who came into the Harbor following the Second World War, pushed out the European immigrants and their progeny, both from certain jobs and from most neighborhoods. In a sense, the 1919 steel strikers, most of them foreign-born, were the instruments of their own ultimate displacement.

Although it hastened the Twin City's maturation, World War I accelerated a variety of other problems that erupted after the war. The combination of its ethnicity, its boom town nature, and the fact that males outnumbered females two to one contributed to the so-called liberal social pattern with its perceived evils. To these were added health problems, some traceable to a municipal water system that had become inadequate; one out of every six infants under the age of two years died of diarrhea or enteritis, and others died of typhoid. Despite a pesthouse (boxcar) on the canal to which victims were exiled, contagious diseases killed many. During the 1921 smallpox epidemic, health officials quarantined some twelve thousand persons in the vicinity of the Twin City. Moreover, barbarous illiteracy prevailed, as people who could not read or write continued to flow into the Twin City faster than the heroic schools could educate them. Immediately after World War I, the Twin City was the most illiterate city in the nation. Economically, the postwar era brought disappointment and gloom. The combination of the 1919 steel strike and the 1921 depression fatally wounded the two largest mills in East Chicago, and they eventually closed permanently. Politically, the postwar period was an impossible time to run the Twin City; applying the new Prohibition law to people raised in countries where drinking spirits was more normal than drinking milk manufactured crime rather than prevented it.

Amidst the squalor of postwar problems, the worst mess was found in the political arena, where a 1921 alley fight became the dirtiest mayoral election in the history of the Twin City, and a metaphor for the self-destructive period following the war. Frank Callahan, a Democrat who had become mayor in 1913 on the Citizens' ticket, this time ran as an Independent. John Kalman Reppa, a banker and the city controller, ran as a Republican. With no holds barred, the rhetoric of their respective supporters descended to such imaginative lows that it sparked a local civil war. Friends turned against friends, family members turned against family members, and the governor put the militia on alert. Chief loser in the fray, however, was the Twin City *Sentinel*, the community's first and only daily newspaper, which backed the wrong candidate. During the early morning following the election, the newspaper shop received an unscheduled visit from a group of sore winners, smartly attired in suits, masks, revolvers, and sledge hammers. In minutes, the visitors turned the *Sentinel* plant into a chop-shop, reducing every suggestion of equipment to scrap.

This scene outside the Inland Steel plant became a storm center during the Great Steel Strike of 1919. Inland Steel kept operating during the strike, but striking workers attacked workers who tried to enter the plant. To counter this interference, Inland set up cots inside the plant. Clipping from the Chicago Daily News

From a few barracks for strikebreakers in 1919, Mexicans expanded just outside of the Inland gate into a five thousand person colony within Indiana Harbor. Loyal to the country of their origin, the Mexicans preserved their culture with art shows, theater, and even a newspaper shown here named El Amigo del Hogar. *Photo from the East Chicago Historical Society*

To deal with social problems among the foreign-born that had worsened during World War I, the Baptists established Katherine House in the heart of what was once called Hunkeytown. One of the most important institutions ever created in the Twin City, Katherine House shied from no problem, whether of health or juvenile delinquency or education or Americanization. Ironically, Katherine House opened the same day that the Great Steel Strike of 1919 exploded. On hand for the official opening was Katherine Westfall, for whom the neighborhood house is named. She is the woman in the dark dress standing in the third row to the right of center. Photo from the East Chicago Historical Society

Given its predominantly foreign-born population brought up on spirits of various kinds and strengths, the Twin City was a frequent target of raids by Prohibition agents, shown here alongside city hall with one of their hauls. The impossibility of enforcing the Prohibition laws in the Twin City resulted in the conviction of two police chiefs, the resignation of a judge, the withdrawal of one mayor from an election and the conviction of another, the arrest of the manager of the public docks, and the arrest of hundreds of other Twin City residents, a fraction of the population that was in some way ignoring the law. Photo from the East Chicago Historical Society

Since the Ku Klux Klan opposed blacks, Catholics, Jews, and the foreign-born, they found few recruits in the Twin City. Except in a few churches with heavy memberships of whites from the rural South, people sympathetic to the KKK had to go to neighboring towns for Klan fellowship. Here the Klan performs one of its rituals at nearby Ridge Lawn Cemetery, Gary, in 1925. Photo from the Calumet Regional Archives, Indiana University Northwest

The Twin City's most famous journalist was a woman, an internationally-known reporter who became a casualty of a Twin City political war. As a foreign correspondent in 1900, Marion Heath Freeman, shown here about that time, covered an uprising in Costa Rica for the Chicago Inter Ocean *and other* Chicago papers. *An arbiter of taste in the performing arts, she also spent two years in New York as an advance dramatic reviewer for the* Chicago Journal. *When Sidmond McHie started the* Lake County Times *in 1906 with the avowed intention of making it a big-time newspaper, he lured the famous Hugh E. Keough ("Hek" of the Tribune) to Hammond as editor and Marion Heath Freeman as associate editor. Mrs. Freeman gradually gravitated to the booming Twin City when her husband Joseph took over the East Chicago and Indiana Harbor edition of the* Lake County Times, *while also representing all Chicago papers in the Twin City both editorially and in circulation. In 1908, the Freemans moved from Chicago to East Chicago on Beacon Street, and in 1913 they bought the* Twin City Sentinel, *Joseph handling the business side and Marion the editorial side. When well-dressed hoodlums destroyed the* Sentinel *plant following the 1921 mayoral election, they bankrupted the newspaper. Shortly thereafter, Joseph Freeman's health broke down, and Marion Freeman returned to newspaper work in Chicago, eventually as a columnist for the* Chicago Daily News. *Photo from the Abigal Smith Collection*

The Twenties: Workshop of America

The Twin City reached its zenith between the recovery from the 1921 Depression and the 1929 Crash. It became a world port, its stores flourished, its parks expanded, its chamber of commerce reorganized and became the strongest in the state, it regularly attracted nationally-prominent speakers to fortnightly forums, its industry expanded to make the Twin City the nation's foremost producer of steel and gasoline, it built a hospital, it built its first two skyscrapers, it created new civic organizations, it made city planning a reality, it replaced one high school and built another from scratch, and its citizens felt confident about themselves and their community as never before or since.

So renowned did the community become that in 1928 the Baltimore and Ohio Railroad added to the Capitol Limited, its crack train between Chicago, Washington, D.C., and New York, a handsome new Pullman car bearing the name "East Chicago." Local observers felt this an especially appropriate gesture because it had been on the Capitol Limited that East Chicago and Calumet Region boosters had gone to Washington the previous year to persuade President Coolidge to visit the Region. Ironically, though, because of the Twin City's proximity to Chicago, the B & O scheduled no stop of the Capitol Limited in the Twin City, and so residents traveling to the East had to first travel to Chicago to board what they considered to be their own car. Most of these travelers, however, regarded this as a temporary inconvenience. Given the continual growth in size and importance of the Twin City and the Calumet Region, and given the growing number of local residents traveling to the nation's capital and other eastern points, local leaders felt it would be only a matter of time until the B & O would be compelled to stop in Indiana Harbor.

Fundamentally, the Twin City in the twenties was just about the best place in America to work. Ideally located for assembling raw materials and distributing finished products, the Twin City became a magnet for industries and workers, inspiring a saying that spread across the nation: "If you can't make a buck in East Chicago or Indiana Harbor you can't make a nickle anywhere else." Within only a little more than eleven square miles, fifty industries employed more than twenty-five thousand persons. Twin City industry featured the world's largest miscellaneous foundry, part of the world's largest complete oil refinery, the world's largest cement plant, and the basis for what would be the world's largest steel mill. This massive concentration of industry provided the post-World War I world with a sizeable share of the materials with which it remade itself. In the years following World War I, the Twin City became the nerve center of the Calumet Region, which in just a single generation emerged as the industrial successor to Pittsburgh and the German Ruhr.

After righting itself from the convulsive postwar period, the nation's arsenal of World War I re-blossomed bigger and better than ever. By the mid-1920s, there was no industrial concentration in America more comprehensive than that in the Twin City. From the smelting of iron ore to rolled products, the Twin City annually produced some two million tons of steel, manufactured by four companies. Scrap collection, a large part of steel produced, became a highly organized industry, represented by one large plant. Five iron and steel foundries converted pig iron and scrap into castings. Eight companies fabricated into more highly finished form rolled steel products, such as bars, plates, shapes, and sheets. One firm specialized in the manufacture of high grade valves. Two others made standard valves, pipe, fittings, and accessory products in both cast iron and steel. And four specialty manufacturing firms produced machinery made mainly of iron or steel. Another company, the nation's largest producer in its field, made fire brick, essential in making steel. The world's largest plant of its kind, referred to earlier, produced cement, the base of concrete, the second (to steel) most widely-used construction material. Four plants extensively produced and refined nonferrous metals. Three plants (with two more on the horizon) produced petroleum derivatives, such as gasoline, lubricants, and countless other products. Two companies produced, collected, and distributed the by-products of gas. And two plants, in response to an enormous postwar demand, produced oxygen for cutting and welding metals. In addition to these plants, one large plant produced chemicals, and six other plants manufactured a variety of other products.

Although steel and oil drove local industry, the diversity of Twin City products in the twenties was amazing:

Products	Company
Iron, steel, and fabricated steel	Inland Steel Company
Wrought steel pipe, plates, tin, coke, and coke by-products	Youngstown Sheet and Tube Company
Railroad and tank cars	General American Tank Car Company
Marine, railroad, and automotive forgings	Standard Forgings Company
Bar iron and alloy steel	Interstate Iron and Steel Company
Foundry products:	
miscellaneous castings	American Steel Foundries
gray iron castings, patterns, and machine work	Calumet Foundry and Machine Company
castings and rolls	Hubbard Steel Foundry
Lead	International Lead Refining Company
	U.S.S. Lead Refinery
Steel and structural rivets	Champion Rivet Company
Valves	Edward Valve Manufacturing Company
Bailing presses	Famous Manufacturing Company
Power plant machinery	Green Engineering Company
Steel plates and water purifying equipment	Graver Corporation
Railway equipment	O. F. Jordan Company
Crates, box shooks, and tin plate boxes	Indiana Box Company
New and relaying rails	Hyman Michaels
Wrought washers and carriage	E. B. Lanman Company
Smelters and refined brass	R. Lavin and Son
Pipe fittings	George B. Limbert Company
Superheaters for locomotives and marine engines	Superheater Company

Products	Company
Culverts and traffic signs	Union Iron Products Company
Soft drinks	Nehi Bottling Company
Oxygen	Acme Oxy Acetylene Company
Recovery products (from scrap metals)	Metal and Termit Company
Aluminum	U.S. Reduction Company
Diversified industrial supplies and equipment	Republic Equipment and Supply Co.
Insulation	Weber Insulations, Inc.
Petroleum products	Empire Refining Company (Cities Service)
	Roxana Petroleum (Shell Oil)
	Bartles-Maguire Company
	Sinclair Refining Company
	Standard Oil Company, of Whiting
Cargo transfers	East Chicago Dock Terminal Company
Plumbing fixtures (distribution)	Crane Company
Bricks (for coke ovens and open hearth furnaces)	Harbison-Walker Refractories Company
Self-locking car seals	Dickey Manufacturing Company
Cleaner and other products	Cudahy Packing Company
Chemicals	Grasselli Chemical Company
Cement	Universal Portland Cement Company
Gypsum	U.S. Gypsum Company
Gas and electricity	Northern Indiana Public Service Company
Clothing	Given Clothing Company

107

A Seven Year Celebration

The spectacular growth of the Twin City in the twenties sprang from the fact that the community was located, in the words of a chamber of commerce motto, "where rail and water meet." That strategic position was greatly enhanced in 1927 when the Twin City was blessed with its *second* harbor. Formally opened by Vice President Charles G. Dawes, Buffington Harbor started a new era in the movement of cement from the Twin City. From that day forward, the Universal Portland Cement Company was able to receive by boat and store large quantities of raw materials, and to ship cement by water and rail to all points on the Great Lakes and from them everywhere in the Mississippi Valley. As with all civic celebrations, thousands of Twin City residents appeared for the harbor's opening, which featured the unloading of two boats loaded with limestone from Michigan. In addition, two chartered passenger steamships brought dignitaries in from Chicago's Municipal (Navy) Pier. Among the group present for the opening was E. J. Buffington himself, who had been president of the Illinois Steel Company since 1899. Not only was the harbor named for Buffington, but the nearby railroad station, the post office, and the surrounding territory (once known as Edgemore) carried his name.

Each new industry or expansion of existing industry during the lucky seven years of the twenties added to the wide-spread belief among Twin City residents that there was no limit to what their community could achieve. But perhaps nothing during that golden era gave the community's raging fires of optimism such a blast of air as the Twin City's emergence as a world port. By the end of 1925, the traffic for the port of Indiana Harbor had increased to such an extent that it represented some 4 percent of the combined traffic tonnage of all ports on the Great Lakes, and more than 1 percent of all foreign and domestic waterborne commerce of the United States. Traffic at the Port of Indiana Harbor exceeded such well-known American ports as Providence, Savannah, Jacksonville, Mobile, Beaumont, Erie, Tacoma, and San Diego. Indeed, Indiana Harbor water commerce at that time was twice that of the harbor at Chicago, including the Chicago River. But prior to 1928, a user of the Indiana Harbor Ship Canal had to be located right on the canal. That changed with the appearance of the East Chicago Dock Terminal Company, which bought sixteen acres at the fork of the canal, and took an option for seventy-seven more. There the company installed concrete docks, railroad tracks, gantry and locomotive cranes, and all other equipment needed to load and unload bulk cargoes of steel, ore, scrap iron, sulphur, sand, and other products. By means of eight railroads that ran through the property, the docks also connected with twenty-two railroads entering Chicago. Thus, the docks offered quick transfer in and out of Chicago by both boat and rail. The presence of the docks contributed greatly to a sixfold increase in the freight handled by Indiana Harbor from 1922 to 1929, and to a further enrichment of its population, the result of many sailors jumping ship in Indiana Harbor. The Twin City became a world port in the spring of 1928, when the first ocean-going vessel unloaded its cargo. Naturally, a good part of the community showed up to celebrate.

Whenever the Twin City attained a goal it had set for itself, it marked the moment with a spirited celebration that involved virtually everyone in town. When improvements on Michigan Avenue in Indiana Harbor were completed, for example, the city held a three-day street festival. Begun each evening at seven o'clock with exploding bombs, the festival marked a new era in affairs of the city. Specifically, the festival celebrated removal of streetcar tracks and overhead wires, the paving of the entire business section part of the street, and the installation of a great whiteway system of street lighting. In an atmosphere of a gaudily-decorated Michigan Avenue where merchants happily passed out souvenirs, people milled, listened to concerts, and danced under the blaze of the new street lights for three September nights. Participants had a choice of two concerts. Each evening, the East Chicago Municipal Band performed at the Four Corners, while the Mexican Labor Band held forth at Michigan and Parrish avenues. Later in the evening, the ever-popular Twin City Night Hawks dance band played while revelers swung and swayed in a roped-off section of the street. Other entertainment consisted of circus and vaudeville acts.

Some civic celebrations became institutionalized in the twenties under Cecil Austin, who headed the new recreation department. Every holiday was a reason for Twin City residents to celebrate their good luck of living in such a blessed community. Austin's holiday celebrations included an Easter Egg Hunt, May Day Fetes (with crowning of the Queen by Mayor Hale), a Memorial Day program, a spectacular Fourth of July bash, a program at which John W. Lees had the children as his guests at Lees Park each year, a Labor Day parade and all-day picnic, a Lantern Parade at Halloween, plus Thanksgiving and Christmas programs. Naturally, the biggest celebration was Labor Day, which celebrated what the Twin City was all about.

In 1927, the Labor Day celebration attracted people from throughout the Calumet Region and reached proportions that are difficult to imagine today. It began early in the morning with a parade, organized by George Huish, that included an incredible 586 floats and other vehicles! The procession stretched for three miles, and took a full hour to pass a given point. Most industries and merchants participated, as did such organizations as the White Eagle Club, the Goodfellows Club, the Blue Cross and five other Mexican societies, all branches of the Moose lodge, and the Calumet Specific Club. The O. F. Jordan Company won the prize for the best float. An eleven o'clock baseball game followed the parade and opened the picnic phase of the celebration. After the game, a series of picnic stunts and races were run off under the direction of Roy W. Feik, assisted by H. H. Hutchinson, and these in turn were followed by a second baseball game.

In the evening, boxing took center stage, and in the main bout, Mickey Patrick, an East Chicago boy, won the decision over Spug Myers. Meanwhile, the Mexican Labor Band performed a concert that was interspersed with stage acts. Among other performers, dancers from the schools of Madam Sherpetosky and of Irene Frisbie supplied several numbers. The stage show climaxed with a stirring labor oration. Following the speech, from seven until eleven o'clock, there was social dancing on the clay tennis courts in which hundreds took part. During that time, spectacular fireworks lit up the sky, the show starting at 8:45 and lasting a full hour! An American flag and a falls piece were the two set displays, and a barrage of bombs, rockets, fountains, and other formations were set off. This attraction ended the program for the children.

In many ways, the Labor Day celebration symbolized the

buoyant spirit of the Twin City in the twenties. It was a truly civic enterprise, sponsored by the city and supported by Twin City Post 266 of the American Legion. Its prime purpose was to honor labor, but it did so in such a way as to give community spirit a chance to express itself, both through the committees responsible for its execution and in the participation of the people at large. By amusing and entertaining the populace, the Labor Day celebration, the largest celebration in northern Indiana, kept the people of the Twin City at home. And, in those days where everything paid its own way, the Labor Day celebration, through refreshment and concession sales, made a profit, which paid for the following year's Fourth of July celebration.

Not only did the Twin City celebrate itself in special events and holidays, it celebrated itself in print. The good times and the good feeling about the Twin City manifested themselves in a slick, well-written, new magazine called *East Chicago* (and later *East Chicagoan*), which frankly advertised the Twin City at home and abroad. Distributed not only to chamber members and to other chambers, *East Chicago* was sent to major press clipping bureaus, national advertisers, and newspapers all over the country, and not infrequently it generated coverage about the bullish happenings occurring in the Twin City. The magazine was based on the belief that since the Twin City was in the heart of the world's greatest industrial region, it held a natural and irresistible advantage over all American cities. It sought to let the world know that the Twin City was located on two of the nation's finest harbors, one that did more business than many ocean ports, and on the route of through trunk line railroads. That made the Twin City easily accessible to the ore beds of the Lake Superior region and coal fields of Indiana, Illinois, West Virginia, and Kentucky. And the magazine fairly trumpeted the fact that fifty large industries had located in the Twin City, and implied that any corporation in its right mind would do the same.

The most spectacular celebration of good fortune, as well as an expression of Twin City optimism and pride, was the Greater East Chicago-Indiana Harbor Exposition. Held just south of Washington Park in an enormous tent larger than a football field, the expo showcased East Chicago products. (For the occasion, the grounds were equipped with all public conveniences, such as lights and power, telephones, and plumbing.) Despite inclement weather the first year in 1927, more than thirty-five thousand people visited the exposition during its run of a week in the Fall. Seventy-eight exhibitors, representing every business, industry, and civic enterprise in the Twin City, occupied one hundred booths. Exhibitors lured people into their booths with novelties, valuable prizes, and other devices, and the more enterprising used The Indiana Male Quartet, which was on the general program, to draw particular attention to their booths. The second expo in 1928 had even more exhibitors, more audience, and an even larger tent that covered practically a city block. Two fourteen-piece orchestras on stages at opposite ends of the tent took turns entertaining the huge crowd, and the ubiquitous male quartet was everywhere. Given the success of the first year, clothing merchants trotted out their finest goods to prove that their wares equaled in quality, price, and value, anything in the Calumet Region. The expo also took on the characteristics of an auto show. The center of the tent area was given over to auto dealers who displayed every type of automobile sold in the Twin

City. In a day when most people attending the expo did not own autos but contemplated them, it was an unprecedented opportunity to make comparisons. The automobile even carried over to the main expo prizes: a Ford coupe, a Chevrolet coach, and a 1929 Studebaker Dictator sedan.

A Most Livable Place

During the twenties, the Twin City became the most livable of industrial communities. This condition began with housing, which from the beginning had been inadequate and in short supply. In the twenties, however, elegant homes, apartments, lawns, and parks began to spring up, and neighborhoods generally improved in appearance. This was a considerable accomplishment, because transforming what some people called a waste of sand into a garden spot entailed hauling in and resurfacing the entire city with black dirt, and fertilizing trees in such a way that they would take root under the deep sand. Meanwhile, two industrial housing projects, Marktown and Sunnyside, raised residential standards to a new level.

Marktown, begun during the war in 1917, was the creation of Howard Shaw, a renowned architect whom Clayton Mark had sent to Europe to study industrial communities. Although Shaw modeled Marktown after those communities, he had his own ideas. Instead of rows of dwellings, he designed homes of different sizes and provided for a school (five grades), shops, recreation, club facilities, and free shuttle buses to Indiana Harbor. A discrete community physically separated from East Chicago by the west leg of the canal, and from Indiana Harbor by the main leg of the canal, Marktown consisted of some two hundred white stucco single and duplex homes, a hotel, garage, and four store buildings with apartments above. There were also baseball and football fields, a tennis court, and a playground for the children. Rented to workers of Mark Manufacturing Company and ultimately the Youngstown Sheet and Tube Company for low rates, the buildings and lawns were maintained by the steel company. (In 1942, the homes were sold to Marktown residents.) The hotel rooms were rented exclusively to men, but the dining room was open to everyone and was a tasteful room in which patrons were served by white-jacketed Filipino waiters. A large room in the hotel was used by several churches and other groups. A fountain and park on Dickey Road and 129th formed a circle. (When the road was straightened in 1939, most of the park was removed.)

In 1920, the need for housing for Inland Steel's supervisory employees had become so apparent that the company began to build Sunnyside, a park-like subdivision of one hundred duplexes. Sunnyside served a variety of functions in alleviating the Twin City's housing problem. Like Marktown, it substantially raised community standards for housing. Unlike Marktown, which was on a remote site, Sunnyside was located adjacent to existing housing. Moreover, Sunnyside also broke into land that had been withdrawn from the market during the Baldwin boom, land south of 140th Street. And there appeared more to come. Although Inland built Sunnyside on twenty-eight acres, its real estate subsidiary, Indiana Harbor Homes Company, actually bought 339 acres of land from the Philadelphia Land Company, most of the remaining unplatted land in Indiana Harbor. This offered the hope that new and better housing would finally be built. Except for sidewalks that ran through the prairie however, most of this land would stand vacant for another four decades.

Apart from Marktown and Sunnyside, the promise of attractive housing grew brighter when two new additions to the Twin City were laid out and lots offered for sale. In 1926, 115 residential lots in the Kosciusko Addition and 193 residential and 39 business lots in the Roxana Addition were offered for sale. More basic industrial housing, but nevertheless housing, included seventeen buildings owned by the Harbison-Walker Refractories Company, in the Calumet section. They housed twenty-three families and six individuals, and had a capacity of more than 120 people. In the same vicinity, International Lead Refining maintained a bunk house for emergencies. Inland Steel maintained two bunk houses near its plant, and also owned two rooming houses with boarding facilities in a separate building, which it held in reserve for emergencies.

Along with the general improvement of housing came a drive to improve neighborhoods. This took the form of a beautification movement aimed at transforming the somberness of an industrial community into the brightness of a beauty spot that featured green lawns, flowers, shrubbery, and tree-lined streets. It began with a clean-up and paint-up campaign and broadened from there. Launched in 1926 with a proclamation from Mayor Raleigh P. Hale, the broadened program entailed planting trees along every street in the city. E. A. Kanst, a landscape gardener, surveyed the city and concluded that seventy-five hundred trees of particular types were required. Individual property owners could order the trees from the chamber. Even industries and railroads participated. By 1927, the beautification gathered such momentum that an incredible three thousand tons of dirt and rubbish was removed from the streets. This represented the combined efforts of residents, Boy Scouts, Girl Scouts, city employees, and volunteers, working under the direction of a voluntary Planning and Beautification Committee. As a special incentive, Mayor Hale presented cash prizes for those doing the best work. As the residential sections of the Twin City became increasingly more attractive, so too did their settings. Two new parks were started in 1919, Tod, named for East Chicago's founder and still president of the East Chicago Company, and Riley, named for Colonel Walter J. Riley for his many contributions to the improvement of the city. In 1924 and 1925, Tod Park added a swimming pool that greatly enhanced its attractiveness.

As an enhancement of its living conditions, the Twin City enjoyed exceptional passenger transportation in the twenties. Residents traveled by the Pennsylvania Railroad, New York Central Railroad, three trolley lines (the Indiana Harbor branch of the South Shore, the Gary Street Railway, and the Hammond, Whiting and East Chicago Railway), five lines of motor buses, and a few private automobiles. Always striving to improve even this extraordinary transportation system, community leaders sought to remove the South Shore tracks from Chicago Avenue. They wanted to relocate the electric interurban one block north, on the right of way of the Baltimore & Ohio Terminal Railroad (nee Chicago and Calumet Terminal). Those early efforts paid off three decades later when the tracks were relocated south of East Chicago's downtown section, much to the displeasure of some local merchants.

The Twin City's poorest transportation in the twenties was by means of its roads. Automobile transportation between parts of town was difficult, and few good roads ran to Chicago. To drive from East Chicago to Indiana Harbor was difficult and sometimes impossible. One Hundred Forty-first Street (Columbus Drive) was not paved from White Oak to Forsyth (Indianapolis), and with disintegrating macadam from there to Kennedy. At the canal, a driver faced the obstacle of a rotting wooden bridge that was usually out of service. Should the driver somehow manage to hurdle the canal, he then faced the New York Central (Indiana Harbor Belt) yards with its fourteen tracks, and no way over or under them. If the driver somehow survived to Sunnyside but still wanted to reach Cline Avenue, he couldn't because the street was not open beyond Sunnyside. Nor was Chicago Avenue open east of Parrish Avenue to Cline. As for Forsyth Avenue, apart from the poorly maintained trolley car tracks that inhibited the flow of traffic, Forsyth also had a wooden bridge in poor condition over the Grand Calumet. South of the river, driving was problematical.

Homegrown Fun

Twin City residents not only worked hard they played hard, and to the extent possible that urge to play was channeled into the Twin City's formal recreation program, which became an enormous one. The city cooperated with many athletic organizations, including a highly successful industrial basketball league of eight teams and an industrial and community baseball league of eight teams. The recreation department also sponsored organizations, such as several harmonica clubs that comprised one hundred boys, in addition to one harmonica and three ukelele clubs for girls. As part of its service, the department provided leaders for three girls clubs and four independent athletic clubs, including two for black groups. Mayor Hale strongly supported black leaders and provided them a community center at Columbia Hall. There, all manner of games, from checkers to basketball were promoted. Various clubs for men, women, and children flourished. Some of this work was done in conjunction with, or as a complement to, work done by officials of the Grasselli Chemical plant.

The importance of working closely with the black community was underlined by the rise in the Calumet Region of the Ku Klux Klan, which was antiNegro, antiCatholic, anti-Jewish, antiforeign, and antiorganized labor, which covered just about everyone in the Twin City. This bias notwithstanding, and notwithstanding the fact that the Klan scored some successes in Hammond, Gary, and other communities of the Calumet Region, the KKK did hold meetings in some Twin City churches in 1923. Fortunately, the KKK's appeal peaked in the first half of the twenties when at one point it technically bought Valparaiso University, the school that had produced most of the Twin City's early lawyers. Nevertheless, the situation between blacks and whites in the Twin City had been tense since the steel strike of 1919 and in the sanguine twenties it was, at best, an arms-length rapprochement. Most blacks lived in pockets of the community near their work: Grasselli (Calumet), American Steel Foundries and the metal refining plants (New Addition and Calumet), and

The Twin City in the twenties became the most livable of industrial communities. Since it had all of the amenities of a metropolis, most of the people who worked in the city between 1921 and 1929 lived in it. Until Chicago tired of reform in the mid-twenties, the Twin City even presented Chicago's top boxing cards, including championship fights, at the six thousand-seat Oswego Arena. Squinters can find it in the upper right hand corner, across from the new Roosevelt High School. Photo from the East Chicago Chamber of Commerce

Mayor Raleigh P. Hale, M.D., preached and practiced a doctrine of civic unity and betterment. He introduced system and efficiency to city government, worked for and got needed community facilities and services, promoted hometown activities and entertainment, and introduced city planning. Most of his accomplishments endure to this very day. So does the memory of his exit. In October, 1929, a grand jury indicted Hale for conspiring to violate the Prohibition laws, which only endeared him to many Twin City voters. The following month, they returned Mayor Hale to office. Photo from the East Chicago Chamber of Commerce

Inland Steel (Block-Pennsy). And when Columbus School was started in the New Addition during the late twenties (finished in 1930), the school administration had to be at great pains to assure the public that it was not a segregated school.

Apart from sponsoring organizations that fostered civic unity, the Twin City in the twenties also got into the entertainment business, and used it to cross-promote other groups that benefited the city. For one, the recreation department sponsored the Community Players, an acting group headed by Bernard Friedman and starring J. Edwin Jacobs and Max Friedman. The Players often performed before packed houses, including the 785-seat Forsyth Theater. Among its six yearly plays, the group presented one for the benefit of the Lions Club's Girl Scout Camp project, which cleared more than a thousand dollars. And shortly after Christmas, 1926, the group gave a benefit performance for the Carmalite Home for Girls.

As the Music Man among communities in the Calumet Region, the Twin City sponsored most musical organizations not part of the schools or local lodges. One of the musical groups was The Community Quartet, recognized as the finest amateur quartet in the Midwest. It regularly performed on station KYW and was in great demand at local affairs. Most visible of the Twin City's music organizations in the twenties was the East Chicago Municipal Band, managed by Al G. Perry, directed by Albert Cook, and funded by the park board, city council, and department of recreation. It debuted on East Chicago Day at the Lake County Fair. Twice each week during the summer, the band entertained at concerts in the parks. During its ten week summer season, the band played concerts every Wednesday night at City Hall Park, where a new band shell had been erected, and every Friday night at Washington Park, which also had a band shell. Besides these programs, the band also played in city parks every holiday, their most elaborate program being on the Fourth of July. A quasi-pops group, the band played standard numbers interspersed with popular selections. Part of a program to provide clean and wholesome alternative entertainment for Twin City residents, the band comprised the finest musicians in the city, augmented by first chairmen who had appeared with some of the world's leading bands.

The Rise of Civic Clubs

The twenties also saw the creation of a number of new civic organizations, and the enlargement of others. The American Legion came into existence in 1919, backed a variety of community projects, and was especially active in seeking homes for the orphans of veterans. The Elks, organized in 1905 by Mayor William F. Hale, older brother of Mayor Raleigh P. Hale, moved into a new home, which was a quantum leap forward in facilities. The first group of twenty-five had met in the Tod Opera House until it burned down, and then in the newly-built Water Building on Olcott Avenue (which in the twenties housed the Knights of Pythias), and then a third story added to the East Chicago Bank building for lodge room purposes. The new building, however, was a combination temple, hotel, and stores, and was one of the finest buildings in the community.

The Lions Club came into existence in 1926, and almost immediately two members donated a two and a half acre site on a lake in Michigan to the Girl Scouts to be used for a camp. They then organized a benefit that netted fifteen hundred dollars to erect a clubhouse, completed in time for summer camp. In 1927, fifty-girl contingents arrived at Camp Echo. In all, 125 girls enjoyed the camp that first year.

The club that had the greatest impact of all, however, was the Kiwanis Club, organized March 31, 1924, with the charter being received by Raleigh P. Hale, the club's first president. During the second month of its existence, the club created a Junior Baseball League for boys not exceeding fifteen years of age. The Kiwanis furnished uniforms and equipment for more than one hundred boys who formed the eight teams in the league. The next summer, the club also sponsored Mostil Day (September 10, 1925), and conveyed all players in the Kiwanis League to Comiskey Park, Chicago. There, the boys dressed in their baseball uniforms, hobnobbed with major leaguers, and received attention from Johnny Mostil himself, the famous White Sox outfielder and pride of Whiting. The East Chicago Kiwanis League is the oldest boys' baseball program in America, and predates Little League by more than two decades.

Far from being limited to baseball, the Kiwanis seemed to participate in every activity that advanced the city. In September of 1925, the club, working with other civic groups, spearheaded East Chicago Day at the Lake County Fair. More than five hundred automobiles, buses, and trucks took some seven thousand people from the Twin City to Crown Point for the biggest such day ever seen at the fair. In addition to the hordes of people who showed up to celebrate their city, there were three bands, including the East Chicago Elks Band (which had just won the state championship at Valparaiso), the celebrated East Chicago Senior High School Band, and the fine East Chicago professional municipal band. As a further declaration of allegiance to their city, the Kiwanis also proposed a name change for the city and, in cooperation with the chamber and the Manufacturers' Association, distributed questionnaires to all civic organizations.

The organization that transcended all others, however, was the chamber of commerce, which reorganized in 1924 and set the pace for community development. It was the common denominator for all things positive in the community, from a new credit bureau to universal tree-planting. The chamber even sparked the community's evolving social services. While chamber members enjoyed their community's euphoria during the twenties, the chamber recognized that not all problems arising from the war and postwar period had been solved. For this reason, in 1924, they organized the Community Chest to make philanthropies of various social organizations more effective. In 1925, the Chest appointed Mrs. Beryl T. Gould, a social worker, as full-time worker in charge of the Emergency Relief department of the association, and a small emergency relief fund was established for temporary relief of all kinds until appropriate authorities could be notified and arrangements made for permanent care. Meanwhile, the chamber cross-supported the Manufacturers Association, led by Colonel Walter J. Riley, which underwrote most of the cost of the city's first city hospital, St. Catherines. It was built on land donated by Inland Steel's Indiana Harbor Homes subsidiary, just east of Washington Park.

Because the chamber was the nerve center of most organiza-

James Thomson, second from right, not only was chief engineer of Hubbard Steel Foundry Company, but also headed the Twin City's relentless planning and beautification committee. A native of Scotland and a devotee of John Muir, America's leading naturalist, Thomson's modest goal was to transform the sooty, sandy Twin City into a bower of greenery, and his program included planting trees along every street and boulevard, improvement of all lawns, and a clean-up of the Twin City that stopped nothing short of the immaculate. He succeeded beyond all reasonable expectations. Alas, Thomson Park, proposed to be built in his honor a block south of Sunnyside, never materialized and remained an unattended waste of sand and weeds throughout most of Thomson's lifetime. He is shown here with his 1927 cleanup chairmen as they receive a charge to make the Twin City sparkle. The man in the campaign hat is Arthur J. Sambrook, executive director of the Boy Scouts, who provided many of the foot soldiers in the war against dirt. Photo from the East Chicago Chamber of Commerce

Girl Scouts, not to be outdone by their male counterparts, marched onward as to war to "Clean, Paint, Plant." Inspired by the Salvation Army band, supplemented by a few musical free-lancers, the combined beautification forces annually collected more than three thousand tons of trash. Photo from the East Chicago Historical Society

tions and community leaders, its support was the support of the entire community, and the chamber used that power on behalf of anything that would improve the community and validate its confidence in itself. One of its campaigns even helped bring a new Superior Court to the Twin City. In 1927, the Indiana legislature transferred Room Two of the Lake Superior Court from Hammond to Indiana Harbor. Until that time, the Twin City had been the largest city in the state without a court of general jurisdiction. The court established itself in the impressive new Odd Fellows Temple, located in a quiet neighborhood at the southeast corner of Broadway and Grand Boulevard. The building itself, like the Elks Temple in East Chicago, was more tangible proof of the rapid rise of the Twin City. Judge Maurice E. Crites, who presided over Lake Superior Court Number Two when it was in Hammond, continued on the bench. Crites was already an Indiana Harbor resident and active in Twin City affairs, especially through the chamber of commerce. For several years, he had been president of the Community Chest.

As the Twin City rode high in the twenties, the chamber also helped the community become the site of many state conventions and special events. Typical of the state conventions was the annual meeting of the Indiana Bankers' Association. Approximately two hundred bankers from all over the state converged on the Twin City for a meeting in the Elks Temple for the eighteenth annual meeting. Besides business sessions and dinner, the visitors toured the Universal Portland Cement plant, played golf, and shot skeet at Whiting Park. The chamber's biggest coup, however, was the visit of President Calvin Coolidge, who arrived at Calumet Station at the beginning of a Region-wide event that climaxed in the President's dedicating Wicker Park. Although 100,000 people attended the dedication, almost that many more lined the parade route along Kennedy Avenue through the Twin City and Hessville.

Although the chamber, especially through its magazine, could at times appear almost smug about the Twin City, its leaders refused to stand pat. Led by C. H. True of Superheater, they wanted a bigger and better city, and so in 1925 the chamber commissioned a survey designed to deal with the community's blemishes and various economic aspects of the city. It, therefore, focused on such matters as the eternal housing shortage, street congestion, railroad relocation, poor highway transportation, tangled railroad tracks, the absence of a department store, inadequate water and sewer systems, large tracts of undeveloped lands, inappropriate taxation for school and civil budgets, parks, community centers, air purification, waterways, Americanization, dreary landscape, lack of a hospital, lack of a cemetery, the failed use of the Grand Calumet River, territorial growth, relations with adjoining cities, and the ambiguous name of the city. Out of the survey came a plan that looked far into the future.

The End of Camelot

Raleigh P. Hale, M.D., the prime force in bringing the Twin City to the heights during the twenties, took office as mayor in 1926. The optimistic new leader headed what many observers consider to be the most effective administration in the history of

the community. Hale unified the Twin City, and gained agreement in principle at least, on a single name for the municipality. He introduced efficiency, with economy in every city department. He implemented a plan for law enforcement that included a well-organized police department with advancements based on a merit system. He introduced a zoning plan and laid the groundwork for adequate highways, featured by the eventual opening of Chicago Avenue across the entire city, the opening of Forsyth Avenue, a full opening of 141st Street (including a viaduct over the New York Central yards in 1929), extension of Michigan Avenue to Chicago Avenue, and the opening of Cline Avenue. He worked for the erection of a hospital, expansion and improvement of parks, and a community center. He promoted new housing and home ownership as well as new and more varied stores. By making the Twin City eminently livable, with so many local attractions that people did not have to go elsewhere to shop or be entertained or find recreation or gain the other extra-material rewards of life, he persuaded most of the people who worked in the Twin City to live there also. During the Hale era, East Chicago, Indiana, became a community in every sense of the word. If ever the Twin City had a booster as mayor, it was Raleigh P. Hale, M.D.

But the twenties was not an easy time to run any American city, and it was an impossible time to run a city where most of the population had been bred to the belief that distillates were essential to a full life. While Prohibition had become the constitutional law of the land following World War I, Twin City residents could not believe it applied to them. Born and raised in countries where drinking spirits was more normal than drinking milk, the immigrants continued to buy and make their own hootch, in the manner of their responsible forefathers. It seemed ludicrous to them that one of the normal rhythms of life should be arbitrarily interrupted. Nevertheless, a law had to be honored and the less abstemious locals did so by adding to the art of spirit-making the art of surreption. Overnight, persons accomplished in the game of "hide the hootch" gained added status in the Twin City. One of the community's most respected citizens was the undertaker, who co-mingled the forbidden nectar with his customary cargo, moving both about town in his hearse. Nevertheless, in 1921 the government began to seriously challenge Twin City customs, and to try to persuade residents that they were not exempt from the Volstead Act. Thus, zealous federal agents swooped into the Twin City anticipating a link-up with local police for a quick strike against the forces of wetness. Since such confiscatory action opposed the popular public interest, however, the police chief and his captain simply declined to join the agents in cracking down on local bootleggers. For their service to public sentiment, the police leaders received the gratitude of the more parched of the denizens and two years in a federal penetentiary. Three years later, City Judge Twyman quit, saying that nobody could enforce Prohibition. And when re-election came around again, Mayor Callahan chose not to run for the same reason. That's when kindly Dr. Hale took over.

Being a physician and practical man dedicated to the health of people and a population, and also being a man dedicated to taking his chosen city to the top of all industrial cities, Mayor Hale made a long priority list, referred to earlier, and threw

himself into the task of making the Twin City a good place to not only work but to live and play. He wanted to make his community a great city, not a dry one. Volsteadism did not make his list. Thus, his enthusiasm for his city proved to be his fatal flaw.

The Golden Age of the Twin City ended with two cataclysmic events toward the end of 1929. One event was the stock market crash, whose delayed impact on the city trashed its economy. The other, which climaxed at the same time, was yet another visit by Prohibition agents. Actually, the agents had been in the Twin City since January, taking jobs in the mills and generally becoming invisible in the community where they became acquainted with the fact that more than half its residents were involved in illegal hootch, as makers, runners, or consumers. They made their move in August, when they arrested one hundred twenty-five people, including women, for conspiring to violate the Prohibition law. They confiscated stills, mash, and alcohol, although what they took was a teaspoonful out of the ocean of booze on which the Twin City floated. And they called the Twin City the most wide-open city in the state, which belabored the obvious.

Alas, one of the people the agents caught in their net was Mayor Raleigh P. Hale, M.D., the Lancelot of Camelot who, through his office and through community organizations, had led the Twin City to the crest of its life cycle. They also arrested James W. Regan, the police chief, and others. Within two months, they gained an indictment against not only Hale and Regan, but two hundred others, including the man who had helped make the Twin City a world port—the manager of the East Chicago Dock Terminal, entry point for Canadian booze. Shortly after the grand jury indicted Hale and other community leaders, the citizens of the Twin City went to the polls to elect a mayor. Naturally, they voted Hale back into office. But that did not stop the legal process. In another two months, a federal district court found Hale, Regan, and others guilty, and Hale resigned as mayor. Three months later, Hale and the others were fined and sentenced to two years in Leavenworth. It didn't help much that the following year, the Circuit Court of Appeals reversed the decision, and ordered a retrial. Before the trial could be completed, Hale collapsed and died. The government dropped its case against Regan. But the party was over.

The forces of beautification in one year planted seventy-five hundred trees and seeded untold numbers of lawns and parkways. As trees began to line Twin City streets, the department of public parks each spring sprayed all the trees and shrubs its equipment could reach, and did so free of charge. To help homeowners complete the job, the department distributed bulletins instructing homeowners on how to apply insecticides to bugs most common to the Twin City. In 1929, the department added a special spray service at a nominal cost. That was the year that caterpillars, acting like locusts, descended on the Twin City and practically ate it up. Photo from the East Chicago Chamber of Commerce

Fine homes facing Washington Park in the Park Addition to Indiana Harbor helped attract mill executives and keep them living within the Twin City. Photo from the East Chicago Chamber of Commerce

Marktown's 103 attractive, stucco, low-rent houses, its school, and its stores and recreation grounds induced superintendents, white collar workers, and skilled workers to live close to the plant of Youngstown Sheet and Tube during the twenties. Gleaming white and orderly in its prim isolation, 109-acre Marktown represented industrial housing and living at its very best. Photo from the East Chicago Chamber of Commerce

The home of Judge Maurice E. Crites in the Park Addition is seen through two double rows of poplar sentinels, the entrance to Washington Park. Until recently ravaged by insects, the trees stood at attention in mute dignity for four generations of Harborities, like palace guards protecting one of the Twin City's most valuable assets. Photo from the East Chicago Chamber of Commerce

Washington Park, the lungs of Indiana Harbor and the most used of Twin City parks, gave residents easy access to a different world within steps of their homes. A lush glade amidst a riot of industry, it contained numerous picnic tables, a greenhouse and arboretum, children's playground, baseball field, four tennis courts, lagoon, eighty foot toboggan slide, band shell, and an indoor and outdoor zoo. Each summer, a field day attracted more than four thousand youngsters to the park, which complemented the programs of Washington School (note smokestack) just a block to the north. Photo from the East Chicago Chamber of Commerce

MATERIALS In this BAND STAND DONATED

CALUMET LBR. Cº	MᶜKENZIE HDWE.	INDIANA ELECTRIC SERVICE Cº
WASHINGTON LBR. Cº	SEEHASE HDWE.	YEAGER ELECTRIC Cº
WISCONSIN LBR. Cº	SCHOENBERG HDWE.	INLAND STEEL Cº
IND. HARBOR LBR. Cº	HAYWOOD & BIHL HDWE.	CARLSON'S PAINT Cº

BRANT SIGN Cº

The Municipal Band presented twenty concerts each summer, one weekly for ten summer weeks at band shells in Washington Park, shown here, and City Hall Park. As was the case with many community facilities and services, materials for the shells were donated, with Mayor Hale arranging for the donations. For both shells, the city paid less than eighteen hundred out-of-pocket dollars. Photo from the East Chicago Chamber of Commerce

Charles J. Dahlin presented two deer, native to Mexico, to the Washington Park Zoo in 1926, and by summer the first two fawns born in captivity in Lake County doubled the size of the deer herd. Here Dahlin and the deer pass along 142nd Street as part of an animated float in the huge Labor Day parade. That same year, Marcus Hershcovitz donated a black bear cub, Lincoln Park Superintendent Parker donated five raccoons, and the Twin City Police Department contributed two beautiful red fox to the zoo, which not only attracted people to the park but was an educational resource for Washington School. Photo from the East Chicago Chamber of Commerce

The log cabin shown here in Riley Park was, except for plumbing, built entirely by Boy Scouts who used it as their headquarters. The one-story building contained a large assembly room, office, display room, library, and basement, and was outfitted for cooking. Because of its central location, it also served as an assembly point for various civic improvement projects, such as the fire prevention survey shown here. On April 24, 1929, uniformed scouts and firemen, plus sixty-two insurance field men, inspected every commercial and public building in the Twin City to call attention to hazardous conditions. Photo from the East Chicago Chamber of Commerce

119

Tod Park, largest of Twin City parks and one split by Forsyth Avenue (Indianapolis Boulevard), featured a swimming pool, lagoons, a nine-hole golf course, an athletic field, five tennis courts, children's playground, picnic grounds, skating rink, and special flower beds. In 1930, more than sixteen thousand people used the golf course and more than fifty thousand used the pool. Photo from the East Chicago Chamber of Commerce

The lagoons of Tod Park, along with its nine-hole golf course, outdoor swimming pool, and carefully landscaped grounds gave the campus of the new Roosevelt High School, built in 1924-1925 and seen here in the distance, a Camelot quality and an environment more beautiful than that of most colleges. Photo from the East Chicago Chamber of Commerce

Riley Park in 1919, 6.25 acres in the Calumet section almost entirely surrounded by industry, comprised an athletic field, a children's playground, a concrete wading pool, one clay tennis court, a comfort station, and small perennial gardens. In the winter, the non-standard size athletic field was banked and flooded for ice skating. Photo from the East Chicago Chamber of Commerce

East Chicago's Kosciusko and Tod parks were the major gridirons of the Twin City in the twenties, perhaps foreshadowing the day when the west side of town would dominate high school football, not only in the Twin City, but in the state. One of the teams that brought its primordial skills to these parks was the powerful Nehi team, shown here. Photo from the A. P. Davis Collection

The powerful Twin City Gophers, shown here, were undefeated middleweight champions of the 1921-1922 Chicago Midwest Football League. Another strong team was the East Chicago Dodgers, which clashed with the Gophers in the Armageddon of Twin City football before three thousand fans at Oswego's arena. In the waning minutes, the Dodgers rallied to come within a point of the Gophers, and when Riley of the Dodgers drop-kicked an extra point for a seven to seven tie, it touched off a delirious celebration. The Gophers and Dodgers were direct antecedents of the professional Calumet Indians and All Stars of the 1930s. Photo from the East Chicago Historical Society

Soccer, the favored sport of European immigrants, shared the athletic fields of Washington Park. Here is a Scottish team of the middle twenties. Photo from the East Chicago Historical Society

Largest and finest theater in the Twin City was the Indiana, with a seating capacity of fifteen hundred. Opened in 1926 at 3468 Michigan Avenue, the Indiana combined motion pictures with vaudeville programs. Admission for adults was fifty cents for evening performances and thirty cents for matinees. The theater was well-patronized by people in the American corridor and the Park Addition, as well as by residents of nearby Whiting. Another theater that catered to the American corridor was the Columbia, 3431 Michigan Avenue, with a seating capacity of 472. Photo from the East Chicago Chamber of Commerce

Vacation retreats in the twenties were as close as Cedar Lake, just a half-hour south of the Twin City. Margaret and Archibald McKinlay, recently wed in Pullman, spent a belated honeymoon there. Photo from the East Chicago Historical Society

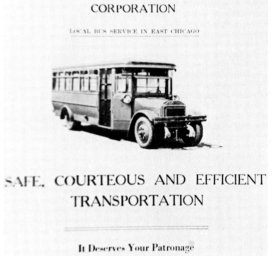

Jitneys would take customers anywhere for a price. In addition to service within the town, the bus could be chartered for special trips, such as conventions, outings, picnics, and funerals. Advertisement from the East Chicago Historical Society

Even a future author of a pictorial history needs a little time off, especially if he can be with his handsome father. From the East Chicago Historical Society

South Shore service in the twenties improved when the railroad rebuilt its roadbed through East Chicago, reduced the time of certain trains into and from Chicago, and added parlor cars and dining cars. Photo from the East Chicago Chamber of Commerce

An ambitious apprentice program began in 1928 aimed at reducing the number of high school dropouts. At the time, more than twelve thousand pupils attended Twin City schools, yet only 150 graduated each year while more than five hundred pupils quit school as soon as they reached the age of sixteen. Apprentices were indentured to individual Twin City plants where they learned the essentials of their trade, and also spent a half day each week at Washington High School in a special class directed by the vocational educational department. Among the eighty-five participants were these apprentices of the Superheater Company. Photo from the East Chicago Chamber of Commerce

Religious education classes, such as the one shown here, were held in Twin City public schools throughout the twenties. Based on the premise that the most impelling force for good behavior is religion, the classes sought to train pupils to be principled men and women by introducing values common to all creeds. Started in the spring of 1919 with ninety pupils enrolled, the program mushroomed to 1,931 by 1927. It was supported by the Community Chest. Photo from the East Chicago Chamber of Commerce

Fred T. Buse tooled around the Twin City each day on his bicycle, personally checking on every pupil absent from school for more than a reasonable time. Not merely the school truant officer, Buse performed a social service function as well. After eliciting the cause of pupils' absences, he served as liaison with various welfare agencies to correct their problems. Photo from the East Chicago Chamber of Commerce

A slick bi-monthly magazine called East Chicago *and then* The East Chicagoan *sang the Twin City's praises from coast to coast. During the late twenties,* East Chicago *was sent to major press clipping bureaus, national advertisers, and newspapers all over the nation. The magazine was based on the modest belief that since the Twin City was the heart of the world's greatest industrial region, it held a natural and irresistible advantage over all American cities. Photo from the East Chicago Historical Society*

125

Important people from all over the world came to see for themselves the phenomenon that was the Twin City. On May 22, 1929, Dr. Rudolph Krohne, minister of transportation for the German republic, inspected the harbor facilities of the Twin City. He arrived with Dr. Werner Schuller, acting German Consul-General of Chicago, and H. N. Roeser, an official of the North German Lloyd Steamship Lines. Alfred Jones (third from right) received them, and H.R. Packard (left), secretary-manager of the Chamber and J.C. Forbes, superintendent of the O. F. Jordan Company, accompanied the visitors. The group is shown here in front of the Calumet Trust and Savings Bank. Photo from the East Chicago Chamber of Commerce

On September 14, 1927, ten thousand proud Twin City residents caravaned in ninety-one buses, some of which are shown here, scores of trucks, and hundreds of automobiles to East Chicago Day, the greatest civic demonstration ever staged at the Lake County Fairgrounds. The event was a combined effort of the Chamber, Lions, Kiwanis, and American Businessmen's clubs, plus the two Women's clubs, American Legion Post 266, and many Foreign-American societies. A parade filled the half-mile track three deep; the Municipal, Washington High School, and Mexican bands played while vaudeville acts and horse racing entertained the crowd. And ethnicity filled the air: George Stoddard, assisted by Tom Costino, arranged for Romanians in peasant costumes to present native dances, while John Tenkely presented a group of Calumet section Hungarians in native costume. Photo from the East Chicago Chamber of Commerce

President Calvin Coolige detrained in the Twin City at Calumet Station on Flag Day, June 14, 1927, to begin a long march to the dedication of Wicker Park in Highland. More than 100,000 people lined the Coolidge parade route through the Calumet section, Hessville, and Highland to Wicker Park. Bands from every community in the vicinity participated in the parade and ceremony. Photo from the East Chicago Chamber of Commerce

The Greater East Chicago-Indiana Harbor Exposition, held September 26 through October 1, 1927 (and repeated in 1928) attracted more than thirty-five thousand people, including eleven thousand the final night, a Saturday. One hundred booths occupied by seventy-eight exhibitors represented virtually every type of business, industrial, and civic enterprise active in the Twin City. The expo was held in a tent that covered practically a city block on the present site of Block Stadium. Photos from the East Chicago Chamber of Commerce

Fortnightly forums that began in 1924 and continued through the twenties, featured outstanding speakers of the day, and gave chamber members insight into both current economic problems and larger movements of the time. Attendance frequently exceeded 250 for subjects that ranged from public health, traffic, and city planning, to conditions in Europe, the Orient, and other foreign lands. Speakers included former governors, clergymen, authors, judges, editors, journalists, poets, engineers, educators, and various other specialists. Here, Speaker Floyd Gibbons, in the fur wraparound, is shown with key chamber members following his 1926 forum presentation. Photo from the East Chicago Chamber of Commerce

The ultimate in boyhood joy occurred when Kiwanis Leaguers from the Twin City met the one and only Sultan of Swat, the Bambino, Babe Ruth himself. This extraordinary experience began earlier with Johnny Mostil Day, September 10, 1925, when the Kiwanis Club conveyed the entire Junior Kiwanis Baseball League to Comiskey Park in Chicago, dressed in their baseball uniforms. For many of them it was their first major league baseball game. Begun in 1924, Twin City Kiwanis baseball is the oldest continuous boys' baseball program in America. Photo from the Sufak and A. P. Davis Collections

In an age when it was fashionable to join and boost, members from various service organizations came together in 1926 for a Civic Week Membership Drive. Workers in the drive are shown here. Photo from the East Chicago Chamber of Commerce

City Hall Park experienced its biggest day ever on October 18, 1926, when the United States Marine Band, "The President's Own," played a free concert for four thousand pupils from the Twin City's public and parochial schools shown here. This free concert was made possible by a sellout for an evening performance given at the new Washington High School Auditorium. The concerts represented a genuine coup for the Twin City. Rarely since the band started its annual tours in 1911 had it stopped in so small a city. The stop was a tribute to the Twin City's importance during World War I as "America's Arsenal" and its continuing importance as "America's Workshop." Photo from the East Chicago Chamber of Commerce

Walter Ballhorn, a German aviator during World War I, came to Indiana Harbor in the twenties and organized the Ballhorn Young People's Orchestra, shown here. Ballhorn supported himself by giving music lessons for twenty-five cents, but if the parents of the youngster could not afford the quarter, he sometimes taught them early Sunday mornings free of charge. Many members of Ballhorn's orchestra went on to play for other Twin City musical organizations, as did Nick Ungarian, the violinist to the left of the drum, who became the band director at Washington High School and an accomplished member of prominent Chicago-area dance bands. Photo from the Young Collection

Civic pride rose to a new high with the performance of the greatest basketball team in the Twin City's history to that point, the 1927-1928 Fighting Senators of Washington High School. The team won an incredible twenty-eight straight regular season and tournament games before falling to Frankfort at the new Butler Field House in Indianapolis. Even then they made the home town proud. Down fifteen to one, the Senators refused to quit and rallied to tie the game at eighteen to eighteen. But that was all they had to give. They fell short, twenty-three to twenty. In the front row were Gansinger, Zeleske, Opasik, Palla, LaPosa, and Walton. In the back row were Sacek, Furticella, Lowalski, Kolina, Coach Frank Cash, Stahlhut, Baran, Widis, and Manager Toth. Photo from the East Chicago Chamber of Commerce

St. Catherine's Hospital, which opened in 1928, was built under the joint auspices of the Manufacturers Association and the Poor Handmaids of Jesus Christ, who also operated the hospital. It was located on long-dormant land bought in 1912 by the Philadelphia Land and Improvement Company, and sold following World War I to the Indiana Harbor Homes Company, an Inland Steel subsidiary. Indiana Harbor Homes sold one city block for the hospital at half the market price, and Inland Steel made the largest single contribution for the building of the hospital. All of the vacant land seen around the hospital was finally built up in the 1960s. Note to the upper right Franklin School, which was built at the same time as the hospital in 1928, to serve children of nearby Sunnyside, a subdivision built a few years earlier by Inland for its supervisory personnel. Photo from the Stuart Thomson Studios

As the Twin City attained its full growth in the twenties, Twin City services also became fully developed, and were coordinated by the Board of Public Works and Safety, shown here garbed in protective covering during an inspection of the Universal Portland Cement plant March 25, 1926. Bottom Row, left to right were H. M. Cohen, board member (and city judge, 1918-1922); W. J. Murray, board member (later a judge); J. H. Kempster, general superintendent, cement plant; C. Stephens, real estate; W. H. Kleppinger, president, Calumet Foundry and Machine Company and Chamber treasurer; and Andrew Rooney, city treasurer (and future mayor). In the top row were F. H. Sass, superintendent of safety and labor, cement plant; E. T. Higgins, president, safety board of East Chicago; H. R. Packard, Chamber secretary and manager; Grover Hansen, superintendent, Grasselli Chemical Company; B. F. Affleck, president, Universal Portland Cement Company; J. S. Dewey, president, public works; H. W. Peterson, city attorney; and Dr. R. P. Hale, mayor. Photo from the East Chicago Chamber of Commerce

Evanson Brothers distributed more fruit, wholesale and retail, during the twenties than any other business in Indiana Harbor. Located at Main and Guthrie streets, the hinge of the old world and the new, Evanson sold fresh produce directly to nearby foreign-born residents and indirectly to native American residents via neighborhood grocery stores. Photo from the East Chicago Chamber of Commerce

George Speros is seen here in 1927 with a colleague in front of his neighborhood grocery store. A sign in the window offering cash coupons suggests that Speros was well out in front of the Green Stamps craze of a later time. Photo from the East Chicago Historical Society

Maurice E. Crites became presiding judge when a new Superior Court was established in Indiana Harbor in 1927. Until that time, the Twin City had been the largest city in the state that did not have a court of general jurisdiction. Photo from the East Chicago Historical Society

The Twin City's first high-rise was the United States National Bank, built in 1927 on the southeast corner of Main Street and Broadway. Seven stories high, the new building was a monument to the progress and prosperity of the Twin City in the twenties. Three floors, including the basement, were occupied by the bank, while the upper floors were used for offices and other purposes. The bank's presence capitalized on and contributed to the development of Main and Broadway as one of the most important traffic centers in Lake County. The bank is shown here about 1940. Photo from the East Chicago Historical Society

Forty-two operators and a total workforce of sixty-two constituted the Twin City telephone exhange in 1926, shown here, which was a long way from where it all started. The telephone did not even appear in East Chicago until 1893, when a pay phone was installed in the residence of Dr. A. G. Schlieker. On December 22, 1899, the first telephone exchange was installed in Max Nassau's jewelry store in the rear of the Sam Cohen Block, and in July, 1902, a separate exchange was established in Indiana Harbor. By 1911, telephones had caught on to such an extent that the Chicago Telephone Company, predecessor of Illinois Bell, erected a building at 908 Chicago Avenue in the Calumet section and merged the two exchanges in it. From mid-1906 to mid-1916, telephones in the Twin City increased from 520 to 2,107, and to 4,281 in mid-1926. Photo from the East Chicago Chamber of Commerce

The East Chicago Dock Terminal Company, organized in 1927, bought and developed fifteen hundred feet at the canal's fork, and installed concrete docks, railroad tracks, gantry and locomotive cranes, and all other equipment needed to load and unload bulk cargoes. With this facility, companies could use the canal without being located on it. Within a year, the Twin City became a world port, as the first ocean-going vessel unloaded its cargo in the presence of a good part of the community. From 1922 to 1929, freight handled in the canal increased sixfold. Drawing from the East Chicago Chamber of Commerce

At nine cents a gallon, filling up the economical new Model A in the twenties meant that a dollar would take a Twin City family as far as it could drive in a week, and leave plenty in the tank for the weekend. Central Garage was located at 819 E. Chicago Avenue. Photo from the East Chicago Historical Society

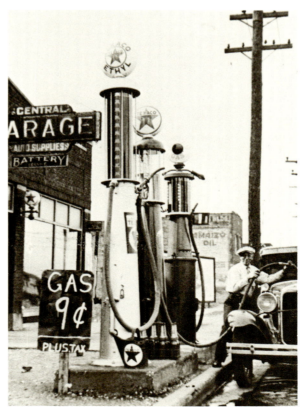

Youngstown Sheet and Tube bought the plant of the Steel and Tube Company of America (nee Mark Manufacturing) in July, 1923, and immediately began to rebuild the plant, tripling its capacity. So extensive was the renovation, shown here in progress, that little remained of the original plant, except the site and even that was increased by extensive filling in of the lakefront. Photo from the East Chicago Chamber of Commerce

Standard Forgings, outlined here in a photo taken in 1967, responded to changes in post World War I transportation and the mechanization of farms by developing the manufacture of drop forgings. It specialized in the heavier types, used principally in the manufacture of automobiles, agricultural machinery, and railroad equipment. Photo from the East Chicago Historical Society

Giant steel pretzels such as these helped make George B. Limbert and Company one of the most successful Twin City enterprises of the twenties. A pipe and fitting company that located in East Chicago in 1903, Limbert had the good fortune to be burned out in 1916 and again in 1920. When it rebuilt, it did so with modern facilities that allowed the company to make products for the high-pressure era of the twenties, when industries demanded piping and fittings capable of withstanding pressures unheard of in the teens. These industries included utilities with their new superpower stations and oil refineries with their new equipment designed to increase the yield of gasoline from crude oil so as to feed an increasingly mobile American population. Photo from the East Chicago Chamber of Commerce

The freighter Eugene J. Buffington is shown discharging cargo during the formal opening in 1927 of Buffington Harbor, the Twin City's second harbor. J. H. Kempster, general superintendent of the cement plant, is inset. In addition to the huge dockside crowd, others who participated in the dedication included Vice President Dawes, who was in the Twin City at practically the same time as President Coolidge. Photo from the East Chicago Chamber of Commerce

The Great Depression

The abrupt change in fortunes from the prosperous twenties to the impoverished thirties left many Twin City residents dreaming of a simpler time. That pensive mood is caught by a member of the McKenna family in this double exposure. Photo from the Stuart Thomson Studios

The Great Depression demoralized the Twin City, and permanently changed its personality. From the supremely confident, almost cocksure amalgam of a hundred races that superintended its own destiny to grow ever bigger and better, the Twin City became a timorous suggestion of itself and hunkered down. Survival, not vigorous vitality, became the priority. The Depression stopped industrial growth, idled thousands of workers, and generally caused the community to live off its assets, which gradually depreciated. People, business, industry, and the city merely endured, not defeated but shorn of the exuberance of the twenties when anything was possible.

In the large sense, the Great Depression in the Twin City was a problem of supply and demand: too great a supply of workers and too small a demand for them. To help solve the problem, American Legion Post 266, one of the forces of Twin City chauvinism and ebullience in the twenties, spearheaded a drive to cut supply. Its plan was simply to pay the way back to Mexico for those Mexicans who wished to go. While latter day sociologists and historians have criticized this event as something akin to the forced re-location of Japanese during World War II, others say that it creatively capitalized on a situation that was already happening.

Deprived of jobs and already on the bottom rung of the Twin City economic ladder, the Mexicans were among the first and the most numerous people to receive relief, which gave them a bare subsistence. Under such circumstances, some members of the colony found little reason to linger, and several hundred who could afford to do so paid their way back to Mexico. As this notion of returning home became popular in the colony, industries provided work sufficient to pay for transporation. At the same time, individual citizens helped other Mexicans return home, and churches began to take special collections to help those who wished to leave. Eventually, the township paid for train fares. As the Depression deepened, however, both private and public funds began to dry up, and many who wished to return to Mexico could not do so. It was at that point that the American Legion proposed a mass repatriation. By the end of 1932, voluntary repatriation had reduced the Twin City's population by some eighteen hundred Mexicans.

The most publicized event of the Great Depression, however, occurred at 2:45 P.M., January 15, 1934, when John Dillinger and Red Hamilton entered the First National Bank in East Chicago. Dillinger carried a trombone case, but did not have a concert in mind. It was a raid so well planned that the intruders even cut the power for the South Shore that ran on Chicago Avenue; Dillinger did not want to be inconvenienced by any passing trains. For his care in the venture, the so-called Hoosier Robin Hood and his colleagues got away with $22,500. Had their research been more thorough, they might have done even better. Not knowing about an elevator that led down to another vault, they left behind a half million dollars.

Although Dillinger took Walter Spencer as hostage, he and his band still had to shoot their way out of town. In the process, they killed patrolman William Patrick O'Malley after several of O'Malley's bullets bounced off Dillinger's bullet-proof vest. It was Dillinger's first killing and it ultimately led to his capture. A bizzare episode ensued at Crown Point jail, which ruined the career of the only Twin City man to come close to occupying the governor's chair. Just prior to Dillinger's escaping from Crown Point jail, allegedly with a gun whittled from wood, a photo taken by Reed Thomson gained wide circulation throughout the state and nation. It showed prosecuting attorney and would-be governor Robert Estill of Indiana Harbor with his arm around the desperado. Poetically, when Dillinger was finally gunned down outside the Biograph Theater in Chicago, he was in the company of an Indiana Harbor entrepreneur named Ana Cumpagnas. A Romanian alien also known as Ana Sage, she is immortalized in the Dillinger legend as the "Lady In Red," the woman who betrayed Robin Hood. She also ran sporting houses both in Gary, where she was known as Katie from the Kostur Hotel, and in Indiana Harbor, a Dillinger haunt and safe town.

From the bottom of the Depression in 1932, the hard times gradually improved until, in 1934, Youngstown and Inland raised the wages of their workers. Both companies, especially Inland, held their workforce in place, and kept thousands off the relief rolls by spreading out the work, cutting work time rather than workers. Meanwhile, various agencies of President Roosevelt's New Deal employed some of the idle men. By the start of 1937, the mills employed more workers—not necessarily full time—than they did in the record year of 1929, and for a fleeting moment in 1937, the nation emerged from the Depression.

Prior to that, however, on August 9, 1936, the Steel Workers Organizing Committee (SWOC) of John L. Lewis' Congress of Industrial Organizations (CIO) established a campaign and recruiting office in Transylvania Hall. Nine months later, SWOC took on Inland and Youngstown and other members of "Little Steel." The strike began in May, 1937, as the mills banked their furnaces, and supervisors and foremen moved into the plants to keep them from closing down completely. Following the so-called Memorial Day Massacre at Republic Steel across the state line in Chicago, five thousand SWOC organizers staged a protest march in Indiana Harbor, marching from the Inland plant gate to the Youngstown plant gate. The five-week strike ended for Inland at mid-year, as workers celebrated all over town. Two weeks later, it ended for Youngstown, seemingly in victory. In fact, though, all the steel mills agreed to was recognition of SWOC as one of several agents representing employees. Meanwhile, work stoppages occurred in the refineries, where unionized oil workers battled each other to determine which union would be recognized. In the end, the union men switched from the American Federation of Labor (AFL) to the CIO, and gradually, most refineries signed contracts with the CIO.

Conceived in the optimism of the twenties, Inland's six-story office building, the Twin City's second high-rise, opened in May, 1930, just a few months after the stock market crash in 1929. It stood throughout the Depression as a visible symbol of hope that the Twin City would once again grow and develop as the hub of the great Calumet Region. Photo from the East Chicago Historical Society

Steel mills in the Twin City that had operated at or near full capacity in 1929 produced less than half as much by the end of 1930, and less than a quarter as much by the end of 1931. At the bottom of the Great Depression in 1932, Inland, Youngstown, shown here at night, and all other Twin City steel mills operated at less than 15 percent of capacity. Photo from the East Chicago Chamber of Commerce

138

A repatriation program in 1932 succeeded in reducing Indiana Harbor's population by some eighteen hundred in seven months. One of the Mexicans who declined free transportation home was V. F. Garza, who arrived in Indiana Harbor from Mexico in 1923, and took over a primitive Mexican chocolate business in 1927. After expanding into processed cheese and then chorizo, a seasoned Mexican sausage, Garza went on to become one of the most successful wholesalers of Mexican food in the Midwest. Photo from the East Chicago Historical Society

Mayor Thomas W. O'Connor, some time between 1930 and 1933, hands the key of the Twin City over to a bemedaled visitor to the Twin City. O'Connor filled most of the unexpired term of Raleigh P. Hale. Photo from the East Chicago Historical Society

Through the gloom of the Depression, Twin City lodges still found time and ways for hi-jinks. Here the Elks in 1933 initiate a class of what appears to be an assembly of politicians, clowns, flashers, and transvestites. Photo from the East Chicago Historical Society

John Dillinger and his gang held up the First National Bank January 15, 1934, and killed patrolman William Patrick O'Malley. After being subsequently captured and incarcerated in the Lake County jail, Dillinger broke out, allegedly with a gun whittled out of wood or soap. Just before the breakout, he posed for this picture taken by Reed Thomson at the jail. From left to right were Sheriff Lillian Holley, her brother, Chief Deputy Sheriff Carroll Holley, Prosecuting Attorney Robert Estill, Dillinger, and East Chicago Police Chief Nicholas Maker. By posing with his arm around Dillinger, Indiana Harbor's Estill ruined his political career. Prior to the photo, he had been considered a possible candidate for governor. Photo from the Stuart Thomson Studios

Mayor Andrew Rooney, city treasurer in the Hale years and elected mayor in 1934, seems to be saying that the world is his bank, or vice versa. Originally from the predominantly Hungarian Calumet section, Rooney was the Twin City's first so-called ethnic mayor. Although he was the last Republican to be mayor of East Chicago, there have been nothing but ethnic mayors ever since. This Andrew Rooney, by the way, was no relation to the Andy Rooney of CBS News fame. Photo from the Stuart Thomsom Studios

The popular Paul Robeson Glee Club was organized by Pauline Shearer in September, 1929, and named for the famous black baritone, Paul Robeson. Made up entirely of black Washington High pupils, its purpose was to further an interest in a musical genre distinctive to black Americans, the negro spiritual. The Robeson Glee Club made appearances at various school assemblies, at churches, and at its own annual spring concert. During the first three years of its existence, Josephine Dawkins served as president. Shown here is the 1931-1932 edition of the Robeson Glee Club. In the bottom row, left to right were Washington, Upshaw, Moore, Simpson, Miss Shearer, director, Josephine Dawkins, president, Hurt, Hudson, McSwain, and Bailey. In the middle row were Hill, Simpson, Doss, Beglar, Harris, Fields, Roberts, Robinson, Tillotson, Dillard, and Starks. In the top row were Johnson, Butler, Stewart, Fields, B. Kilpatrick, Eadon, C. Kilpatrick, Scott; J. Dawkins, Stepliens, and H. Dawkins. Photo from the East Chicago Historical Society

Leaders of the Twin City's extraordinary music tradition included these teachers at Washington High School, seen here in 1933. Seated was Shearer. Standing were Boyce,

Creitz, White, and Mears. Photo from the John McShane Collection

To provide a Depression outlet for graduating seniors with musical talent, Robert J. White in 1930 organized the East Chicago Music League, which under various names he directed until his death in 1955. It began with nine men who gathered for an evening of group singing: Luther E. Burroughs, Eugene Creitz, Russell Gibbs, Herbert Lahr, Lewis Mears, Floyd Merriman, Ray Rutledge, Harlan Walley, and Walter Williams, with Mary Lois Clark as the accompanist. But it quickly came to have three parts, each of which originally consisted mainly of Washington High School alumni. The Civic Orchestra, under the direction of White and Bourroughs, had forty members; the Male Chorus, also under White, had fifty members; and the Women's Chorus, under Pauline M. Shearer and Mary Lois Clark, had about half that number. After singing mainly in churches and small affairs, the league scored its first triumph at the 1933 Music Festival held on May 3, before a large and appreciative audience in the Washington auditorium. Afterward, parts of the league became the Calumet Symphony Orchestra, the East Chicago Male Chorus, and the Farrar Choral Club, all three affiliated with the Calumet Center of Indiana University. The combined groups are shown here in 1936. Robert White is just left of the center gate, and Mary Lois Clark is right of it. Photo from the East Chicago Historical Society

The Calumet Center of Indiana University's Extension Division began in 1932 with offices at Roosevelt High School. By the time the Center moved into this limestone building in Tod Park in 1939, enrollment had increased from 252 students to more than 1,200. Not only did the center provide up to two years of college work and adult education, it also sponsored many cultural activities, such as adult music projects, concerts, work in art, dramatics, public lectures, conferences, and special study groups. Photo from the East Chicago Chamber of Commerce

Jack Albertson, the P.T. Barnum of the Twin City, each week of the Depression found novel ways to persuade residents to spend their scarce loose change on movies at the Indiana Theater. One of the most beneficial of these was a promotion that collected cans of food for the needy, which he conducted in conjunction with Katherine House. Photo from the East Chicago Historical Society

Every Saturday, throngs of Indiana Harbor children spent their entire capital—dimes— on the Kiddie Klub at the Indiana Theater. The "Klub" included a double feature movie, cartoons, short subjects, a thrilling episode of a serial, organ music, group singing (words on the screen with a bouncing ball), prizes, and an amateur hour in which anyone or group in the audience could participate. Winners among the singers and dancers and other performers were chosen by applause, with Jack Albertson holding a dollar bill over each contestant's head, while the audience showed its appreciation. Notice in this photo how Albertson put the first Kiddie Klub on the side of the angels by involving the schools' patrol boys and girls. Photo from the East Chicago Historical Society

Albert Marcus, seen here in the window of his jewelery store, frequently did cross-promotions with Jack Albertson, in this case on the matter of a dishes giveaway. Photo from the East Chicago Historical Society

In the days before the tube, Jack Albertson used the stage of the Indiana Theater to perform the function of today's thirty-second TV spots and PBS programs, and people paid for the privilege of viewing. Here, in a live presentation complete with sponsors, an early-day Julia Child—called a home economist—commanded the attention of a packed house of women eager to learn how to use new major appliances they hoped they might some day be able to afford. Photo from the East Chicago Historical Society

Barnum had his Tom Thumb and Albertson had his miniature Mickey Rooney. Entertainment-starved people lined up at Barker's (another cross-promotion) to catch a free glimpse of a miniature young Tom Edison, which just happened to be the title of a movie playing at the Indiana Theater. The optical illusion they saw playing with test tubes, however, was none other than John Farmer, then a teenage usher at the Indiana Theater, and later one of the Calumet Region's most successful distributors of pipe, valve, and fittings. Photos from the East Chicago Historical Society

6-26-34

Next to fires, accidents drew the biggest crowds during the Depression, when people took diversion wherever and in whatever form they could find it. In 1934, the main attraction in town occurred when this steam locomotive of the Elgin, Joliet & Eastern derailed. Photo from the East Chicago Historical Society

This three-door central fire station on Columbus Drive opened in 1938, complete with a new squad car, thousand-gallon pumper, and seventy-five foot hook-and-ladder. It was this hook-and-ladder that became part of Twin City legend when it overturned in 1938, taking the corner of Euclid and Broadway too fast, while speeding to a fire. The accident killed Vince Szary and injured six others. Naturally, the fire truck was on its way to what turned out to be a false alarm. Photo from the East Chicago Historical Society

Camp Tippy was an early Katherine House camp whose users were sometimes under-written by another organization in the Twin City. Here are Tri Kappa-sponsored campers at Camp Tippy in 1940. Among this group were Pricilla Kazaroff, Gus Bregzis, John Snyder, Hank Zawicki, later a coach, Joe Vargo, later a school administrator, and Ray Krajewski, who later became dean of Calumet College. Photo from the East Chicago Historical Society

The Twin City's recreation department worked overtime during the Depression to keep young people busy and entertained, preferably in activities that cost them little or no money. Rudolph Jarabak, a pharmacist and recreation director, is shown here encouraging fourteen-year-old George Urban, who was an entrant in an early Soap Box Derby, which was run down the west slope of the Columbus Drive viaduct. Photo from the East Chicago Historical Society

146

Each fall, the Chicago Bears opened their season with an exhibition game against the Calumet All Stars. Descendants of the old Gophers and Dodgers, the team comprised recent college stars, such as Jimmy Angelich, Lew Hamity, Vin Oliver, Fred Jaicks, Gene Opasik, and others who passed up professional football for careers in business, industry, and the professions. Jaicks became president and chairman of Inland Steel. Poster from the East Chicago Historical Society

The foxy styles of the Depression are modeled here by Helen Callahan Brown, daughter of a former mayor. Before her marriage, Miss Callahan was a French teacher at Washington High School. Until well after World War II, women had to resign their teaching positions when they married. Photo from the Kathryn Schock Gale Collection

Among the popular young men around the Calumet section in the thirties were, left to right, Johnny Will Thomas, Lee Hart, Andrew Robinson, and C. R. Miller. Photo from the East Chicago Historical Society

Republicans fell from favor during the Depression, never to recover, and those few who were Democrats picked up the pieces and formed the core of a new and enduring political regime. Here is the Twin City's central Democratic Committee in 1938. The man on the left at the end of the second row is Walter Jeorse, who eventually (1952-1964) became a three-term mayor of the Twin City. Photo from the East Chicago Historical Society

Lowell Robertson did field work at Katherine House in 1929 and took over as director just before the depth of the Depression. He ran a variety of health clinics, Americanization classes, clubs, sports leagues, and even farms where people willing to help themselves raised their own food. The Twin City's primary child care nursery still bears Robertson's name. Photo from the East Chicago Historical Society

Frank Migas, who became mayor in 1939, is shown cutting a ribbon at the opening of a fully-paved Chicago Avenue. An American success story, Migas came to Indiana Harbor from Poland in 1906 and, after working for the Charles Martin Baking Company and Inland Steel, he started his own dairy business in 1909. Nine years later, he added candy manufacturing to his business, and the next year he became a director of the People's State Bank in Gary. With the Depression, he became in 1930 chief deputy sheriff for East Chicago, which led to his becoming mayor in 1939. Photo from the East Chicago Historical Society

World War II

Discarding a long-endured survival mode, the Twin City rebounded economically and industrially—if not spiritually—during World War II. Suddenly there were more jobs than people to fill them. Because of wartime restrictions, however, community assets could not be renewed, and as they continued to wear out the community appeared drab and well-used. Still having the template from World War I, the Twin City slipped easily into a wartime mode, and mills established production records virtually every month for four years.

As needed, plants added new capacity, sometimes at a dizzying pace. On March 3, 1942, American Steel Foundries broke ground for its Cast Armor Defense Plant, and began production six months later. In a short time, Cast Armor hired almost six thousand employees, many of them women. Meanwhile, unions took advantage of the wartime mode to make further inroads. Inland and Youngstown dipped their toes into the waters of union recognition in 1941 when, at the behest of the National Labor Relations Board (NLRB), they took a census of union membership within their plants.

After the United States entered the war, the union foreswore strikes, the National War Labor Board began to arbitrate labor disputes, SWOC changed its named to the United Steel Workers of America, and Inland and Youngstown signed their first union contracts. In October, 1942, Superheater workers voted in the United Steel Workers to represent them. And existing mills adjusted their schedules to suit war production. Sinclair, for example, went from a thirty-six-hour work week to a forty-hour week in November, 1942.

Rather quickly, people adjusted to conditions of wartime. They complained hardly at all when gasoline and meat rationing went into effect. Homemakers learned ingenious tricks to stretch rationed food, and victory gardens became almost as essential as the grocery store. Women workers and those men not drafted usually alloted 10 percent of their pay to the purchase of war bonds, 6,724 of 6,994 employees at Youngstown doing so in 1942. Schools drilled pupils on what to do in case of an enemy bombing attack, and replaced physical education classes with physical fitness programs designed to toughen the boys prior to their going into the service. Public transportation experienced a revival, and since no new vehicles could be produced except for the armed services, the Shore Line trotted out vintage busses to accomodate an ever-increasing volume of passengers.

Meanwhile, all blocks of the Twin City organized in a civilian defense effort, each block headed by a "block captain" who wore a white World War I type steel helmet. Each block also installed a flagpole on which to fly the American flag, and near the base of the pole was a display case that listed the men and women of the block who had gone off to war. Service flags with thick red borders around white fields appeared in the windows of homes, with blue stars on the white field indicating the number of servicemen and women the family had seen go to war, and gold stars indicating family members killed fighting for their country.

As was the case following World War I, the end of World War II brought almost immediate labor problems. American Steel Foundries was struck, Inland was picketed, and Cudahy had labor upheaval. An oil strike closed the refineries, and in October 1945, the Navy seized the Shell, Socony-Vacuum and Cities Services plants, over negotiations for an 18 percent hourly wage increase. By November many veterans were returning from the armed forces to find work. In November the U.S. Employment Services East Chicago-Hammond-Whiting offices reported that about a hundred veterans a day were showing up looking for work. And with the institution of the federal government's 52-20 Club for veterans (twenty dollars a week for fifty-two weeks), many ex-servicemen wearing ruptured ducks simply took a year off.

Labor unrest continued to frustrate the Twin City in 1946. A CIO steelworkers strike in January hit Inland Steel, General American, Youngstown Sheet & Tube, Metal & Termit, and Superheater. Strike fever affected not only industry, but the schools. At Washington High, pupils demanded a stadium, and at Riley School, pupils insisted on a larger gymnasium and younger, prettier teachers. Unrest of a different kind also occurred in the community. The growing number of black residents began to assert themselves, demanding to be seated anywhere in local theaters, not just on the right-hand side, and seeking integrated participation in all school events. Racial unrest gave rise to the Anselm Forum, an organization created in 1947, which sought to improve human relations among cultures, races, nationalities, and religions.

Hitler Predicts U. S. Victory

(Hammond Times Photo)

William Patrick Hitler, nephew of Adolf Hitler, predicted victory for the American forces in the war against the Axis powers when he addressed an audience at East Chicago last night in the third of a series of meetings sponsored by the East Chicago Open Forum. Hitler is shown on the left examining a book and speaking to Dr. George E. Francis, Methodist church pastor, who is president of the forum. Young Hitler was born in England and

Adolph Hitler's nephew, William Patrick Hitler, visited the Twin City in 1942, where he spoke to the third meeting of the East Chicago Open Forum. The only living relative of the German fuehrer, the English-born Hitler predicted victory for the American forces in the war against the Axis powers. He is shown here, left, examining a Roosevelt High School scrapbook and talking with Dr. George E. Francis, Methodist church pastor and president of the forum. Photo from the East Chicago Historical Society

America's entry into World War II curtailed the manufacture of many commodities, led to rationing and the regulation of business, and endangered local businesses, many of which failed. This caused the 12:13 Committee of the Chamber, shown here in 1941, to work overtime and adopt survival tactics in behalf of local retailers. Meanwhile the chamber overall involved itself in civilian defense, defense transportation, defense housing, manpower, certificates of war necessity, the War Production Board, gasoline rationing, meetings with government officials, and wartime taxation. Clockwise starting at twelve o'clock were Levin, Abbott, Blumenthal, McCombs, Lewin, Gordon, Huish, Marcus, Manta, Meis, Tarler, and Dressen. Larson is at the hub. Photo from the East Chicago Chamber of Commerce

For the "Fifth War Loan," campaigners took to the street. At the center of the brigade is Colonel Walter J. Riley, who led record-breaking Liberty Bond sales in World War I. Photo from the East Chicago Chamber of Commerce

151

Patriotic rallies took many forms, some of which involved major productions. This rouser, with a large picture of General MacArthur flanked by Miss Liberty and Uncle Sam, was staged in the auditorium of Roosevelt High School. Photo from the Stuart Thomson Studios

School children occasionally trekked from their classrooms to patriotic excercises at the local theaters. Here, pupils from Washington High School offer a hand salute to a huge American flag at the Indiana Theater. Photo from the East Chicago Historical Society

Ordinary vehicles became promotional media for selling war bonds. Here a truck of Joseph Hartley's, an East Chicago pioneer, has been painted red, white, and blue and adorned with the "V" for victory and the "dot-dot-dot-dash" morse code representation of V, as well as being decked out with the Buy War Bonds imperative. Photo from the East Chicago Historical Society

No one promoted the war effort more vigorously than did the American Legion, and no one more winningly than this comely representative of the Legion. Photo from the Stuart Thomson Studios

Most people left at home took war shortages in stride, including this ingenious beer dealer who, when tire and gasoline rationing limited his scope, reverted to non-rubber tires and horsepower. Photo from the East Chicago Historical Society

Actor James Cagney drew a huge crowd of war workers at this Twin City stop on one of his war bond tours. Photo from the Thomson Studios

Reed Thomson, the photographer whose Dillinger photo removed Robert Estill from the gubernatorial race in 1934, was often told he resembled James Cagney. On the Cagney tour, he gave people a chance to judge for themselves. That's Reed on the left. Photo from the Stuart Thomson Studios

The critical shortage of men in the workforce created unprecedented employment opportunities for women, who also created their own social outlets. The Inland Girls' Club, shown here at a costume party, was one of many organizations for working women that flourished during World War II. Photo from the East Chicago Historical Society

Joseph Mosny came to Indiana Harbor in 1901 after his parents bought the second vacant lot sold on Guthrie Street. During World War I, Mosny served in the Student Army Training Corps (SATC), in whose uniform he appears here, and during World War II served as head of the Twin City's friendly draft board. Photo from the East Chicago Historical Society

In war as in peace, the Twin City was run by a few key people in the community who informally and frequently met to adjust the community's course. Shown here is the reigning World War II group of key people. In the front were Fred Gillies, general superintendent of Inland Steel and two unidentified men. In the back were George Huish, publisher and sometimes American Legion commander, Russell F. Robinson, principal of Washington High School and strong force in civic organizations, Rudolph Jarabak, druggist and city recreation director, Roy W. Feik, superintendent of schools and leader of several community groups, unknown, and Herbert Lahr, principal of Roosevelt High School and solo tenor in several adult singing groups. Photo from the East Chicago Historical Society

A major force in preventing juvenile delinquency during World War II was Katherine House, which occupied young people in a variety of positive ways. Here a neighborhood group makes good use of the game room. Ongoing activities of Katherine House included boys' and girls' clubs, handicraft classes, community programs, dramatics (musicales and home talent programs), game rooms, shown here, a library, family night gatherings, non-sectarian religious services, community kitchen, community programs, day nursery for working mothers, baby clinic, venereal disease clinic, summer camps for underprivileged children, and Americanization and citizenship classes. Photo from the East Chicago Historical Society

The largest crowd ever to witness a baseball game at Block Stadium assembled during World War II when a group of Twin City all stars played Great Lakes, a Navy team made up entirely of major leaguers. Although Block Stadium normally seats thirty-five hundred, with extra bleachers that extended down both foul lines the capacity was increased temporarily to ten thousand. Here, Mickey Cochrane, Great Lakes manager and legendary catcher and manager of the Detroit Tigers, shakes hands with George Sufak prior to the game. Part of the overflow crowd can be seen in the background. Photo from the Sufak Collection

The Twin City brightened up after the war with installation of mercury vapor lights. City electrician Eugene Huish, left, supervises this historic illumination on the 3900 block of Main Street in Indiana Harbor. Photo from the East Chicago Chamber of Commerce

As a supplement to the world's largest gas holder, a new, even taller model was installed on the canal east of the Sinclair refinery. Some feeling for the height of this unusual structure can be achieved by comparing the size of the automobiles on the highway with the gas holder. Photos from the Stuart Thomson Studios

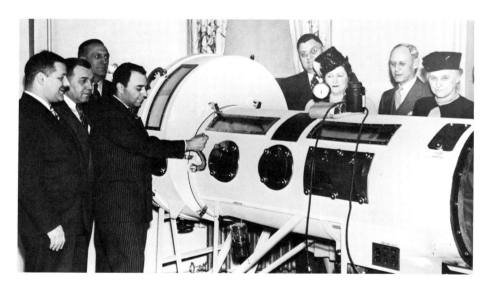

St. Catherine's Hospital began to treat polio victims in 1939, the first and only hospital in the Calumet Region to do so, and continued a strong program through the polio epidemic of the late forties and early fifties. Here a group of community leaders present an iron lung to St. Catherine's. From left to right were Melvin Specter, Al Zivich, Lowell Robertson, Irv Lewin (grasping handle), John L. J. Miller, unknown, Joe Hartley, and Bertha McQuaid. Photo from the East Chicago Historical Society

New industry continued to come into the Twin City right after World War II. Shown here is the assembly line of General American's new Aerocoach manufacturing plant, which produced intercity buses for all of the major carriers. Photo from the Stuart Thomson Studios

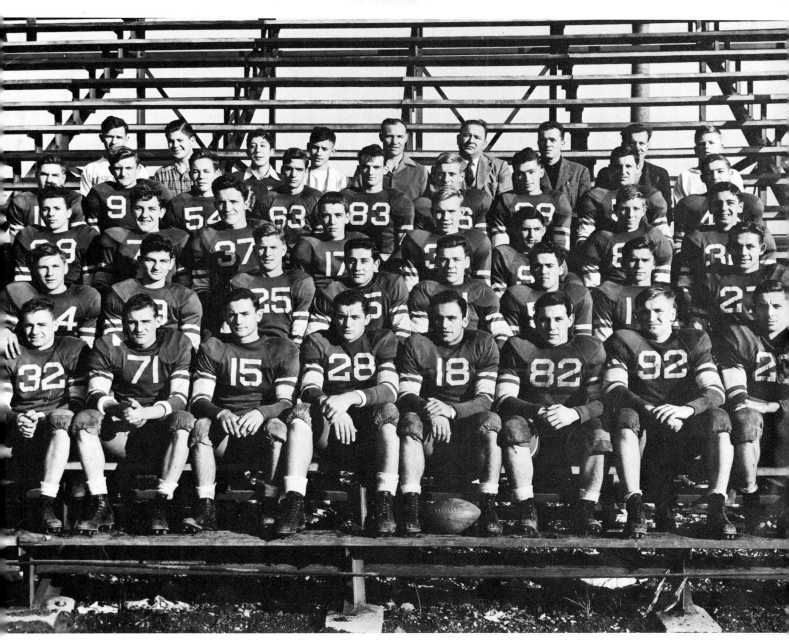

The Pete Rucinski-coached Roosevelt Rough Riders of the forties and fifties compiled a record unmatched by any team in the state, and perhaps the nation. They won or shared eight state championships, went undefeated six times, and once won thirty-four consecutive games. Rucinski, the most successful Indiana high school football coach ever, is in the back row of this photo, third from the right. Fourth from right is John Patrick, athletic director, and next to him is Ernie Miller, assistant coach and the person credited with developing the many outstanding Roosevelt linemen. George Kurteff, third from left in back row, four decades later became first principal of the new East Chicago Central High School. Photo from the Stuart Thomson Studios

The sanguine mood of the fifties was often reflected in industrial Christmas displays, such as this one of Inland Steel. Photo from the East Chicago Historical Society

159

Rabbi Julius Shuback escaped Hitler's Nazi Germany to become the postwar spiritual leader of Beth Sholom. As an eighteen-year old in 1938, he buried his father after the Gestapo murdered him. Some three years later, his mother and sister died in the gas chambers of Auschwitz. Photo from the East Chicago Historical Society

One of the great strengths of Katherine House, and its executive director Lowell Robertson, was that it drew into its orbit virtually all of the community's leaders. Shown here are the Katherine House board of directors in 1951. In the front row were Clifford S. Porter, Earl Gordon, president, Mrs. Kay Havran, secretary, and Mrs. Meyer Levin. In the middle row were Mrs. J. F. McQuaid, Mrs. Hjalmar W. Johnson, Mrs. J. E. Francis, Mrs. Walter Pierazek, Mrs. Benjamin Reese, Mrs. George Kurtz, Mrs. Hattie Leonard, and Mrs. Thomas Morris. In the back rows were Edward J. Johnson, Arnold Eskilson, Erwin Rosenau, Lowell R. Robertson, Kenneth J. Holmes, Jesse W. McAtee, Reverend T. N. Johnson of First Baptist Church, William A. Scott, program worker, Harold Main, Roy H. Larson, F. M. Rich, Inland's general superintendent, Alex Tresnowski, A. Mario Rico, and John P. Fox. Photo from the East Chicago Historical Society

Full employment was the norm during most
of the 1950s, as industry expanded greatly
Photo from the Indianapolis Star Magazine

Everyone pitched in for a good cause, in this case a benefit for the Teen Age Recreation Center, one of Katherine House's several spinoffs. Mayor Walter Jeorse is the head waiter filling up a pot of coffee. Others include, from left to right, Hans Petersen, unknown, Attorney W. Henry Walker, James Hunter, Chub Rich, Mrs. A. Broomes, and Lowell R. Robertson. Photo from the East Chicago Historical Society

The Calumet Art Federated Club, shown here in 1950, was one of several clubs made up of black women. The Twin City Federation of Colored Woman's Clubs coordinated the activities of four groups, which each gave a scholarship to a high school graduate every year. The oldest of the four, the Woman's Improvement Club, was organized in 1921, and the Calumet Art and Welfare Club was formed in 1923. The other two were the Ladies Excelsior Art Club and the Progressive Art and Literary Club. Photo from the Passmore Collection

The Steelworkers Strike of 1959 was the longest on record to that time. Photo from the East Chicago Historical Society

The Twin City solved its major railroad track problem in the mid-fifties when Inland Steel built an overpass over tracks nearest Lake Michigan, transformed Lees Park into a parking lot, and built an all-new park on the B.A.B. of the original lakefront park. At dedication ceremonies, Mayor Waltter M. Jeorse, for whom the park is named, shakes hands with Joseph Block, president of Inland Steel, and namesake of his grandfather and founder of Inland Steel. Under the Joseph Block shown here, Inland Steel reached new heights of prosperity and service to the community. Photo from the East Chicago Historical Society

The last of the South Shore trains on Chicago Avenue ran in the mid-fifties when, in connection with building the Indiana Toll Road, the line was relocated just south of the Grand Calumet River. It was a mixed blessing. While track relocation eliminated traffic congestion, it also inconvenienced passengers who once walked to the train station, and it substantially reduced business activity for some merchants on Chicago Avenue. Photo from the East Chicago Historical Society

St. Joseph's College of Renssalaer began adult evening extension classes in East Chicago in 1951. By 1960, the college was offering a degree program, and within a few years was graduating more than a hundred students annually. Shown here is Raymond Krajewski, academic dean. Photo from the East Chicago Historical Society

The General Electric ambassador of goodwill, shown here in 1956 at a reception preceding a dinner, grew up to be President of the United States. Ronald Reagan was in the Twin City to address the annual meeting of the chamber of commerce. Photo from the Stuart Thomson Studios

The Sam and Henry Indians, shown here in 1956, dominated adult amateur baseball for forty years, starting in 1947. Between 1949 and 1987, the Indians usually won the state championship, frequently won regional midwest championships, and twice finished as runners-up for the national championship. In the front row were Pavich, Kowalsky, Dybzinski, C. Platis, the manager, Estill, Balog, J. Platis, and Morris. In the back row were S. Beneditto, Kijurna, James, Stoyakovich, Gillespie, Stepanovich, Pawenski, Rybicki, Czpczyk, and De Rosa. Photo from the Stuart Thomson Studios

Violet Wradich, a Croatian beauty from Indiana Harbor, represented Indiana in the 1953 Miss America pageant. Photo from the Mason Collection

The 1955 annual Sportsman Banquet for all area high school basketball teams was held at Katherine House. Wilfrid Smith, sports editor for the Chicago Tribune and a former East

Chicago High School three-sport coach was the speaker. He is just to the right of the podium, under the Bishop Noll banner. Photo from the East Chicago Historical Society

RENEWAL, RUST, REBIRTH

The nine-story Lakeview Apartment building looms on the Twin City's otherwise low-rise skyline, a monument to the Purdue/Calumet Development Foundation, engine of Twin City urban renewal. It was dedicated December 4, 1957. As depressed areas of Indiana Harbor were rebuilt, families from substandard dwellings were housed in the building's eighty-six apartments. Lakeview was just one part of the most comprehensive urban renewal program of its kind. Twenty-one industries contributed more than a million dollars in support of the privately-financed foundation program. Notice in the foreground (Turf sign) Colonel Riley's first bank building in Indiana Harbor. It was erected in 1914 a block away at the corner of what became Main and Broadway, and moved in 1928 to what became Pulaski and Broadway so as to make way for a new bank building. Note also across the street the three-story building that was originally known as Tima Burdich's Serbian Saloon and Home. Photo from Inland Steel Company

Renewal

In the 1950s, the Twin City began to renew its well-worn physical assets, depreciated during the Great Depression when there was no capital for investment, during World War II when there were no materials for construction, during the postwar period when community energies focused on peacetime readjustment, and during the Korean Conflict when war priorities again sapped the community's infrastructure.

Renewal began with an aggressive program of improving what already existed. From 1954 through 1959, the Twin City won the National Clean-Up, Paint-Up, Fix-up competition among cities with populations of 50,000 to 100,000 an amazing four times in six years. During the same period, a new gymnasium seating some sixty-five hundred people was added onto Washington High School, which for some three decades then became the site of tournaments that attracted many thousands of visitors to the Twin City. The gym was part of a massive school construction program, during which the Twin City replaced its two pioneer schools, McKinley in East Chicago and Lincoln in Indiana Harbor, while Carrie Gosch School came into existence in Calumet. It also built an administration building where there had been none, and in the mid-sixties, the board of education announced plans to build a Roosevelt High School addition, Joseph L. Block Junior High School, a vocational school (which became the De La Garza Career Center), and the West Side Junior High School. In 1976, the school board awarded a contract for demolition of the old General American office building at 144th and Euclid to make way for a new Washington Elementary School there.

Educational facilities also improved when a branch of St. Joseph College of Rensselaer located in East Chicago in 1951, at first simply as a place to offer evening extension courses to adults. But as enrollment increased, the program offered increasingly more courses until, by the end of the decade, the branch evolved into a college in its own right. In 1960, therefore, St. Joseph's in East Chicago became the first degree-granting college in Lake County since 1865 when Timothy H. Ball established the Crown Point Institute to provide collegiate instruction for young ladies and young men. St. Joseph's graduated its first student in 1961, Mrs. Patricia School of Hobart, and by 1968 had graduated 112. During that time, the campus near East Chicago's Four Corners expanded to include some fifteen buildings covering more than a city block, and became a major cultural resource for the community.

The Twin City also improved its infrastructure in a variety of other ways. In 1954, in a joint project with Inland Steel, it dramatically improved the lakefront. The project yielded an overpass over an annoying and dangerous concentration of trunkline tracks, a new lakefront park, and improvements in the water works. In 1961, the Twin City formally dedicated a new fire station, a new central police station, and a new city court on Columbus Drive at Alder Street. An honored guest was Walter J. Riley, the city's first judge in 1911. Six years later the Twin City built a new main library across the street, on Alder Street. In 1964, the city built a new water plant, replacing one it had bought in 1924 from the East Chicago and Indiana Harbor Water Company, a plant that had its origins in 1893. In the mid-sixties, it also modernized its sewage disposal plant, built in 1945, with equipment capable of meeting the new clean water standards,

and even of recovering oil from the Indiana Harbor Ship Canal. And in 1970, the city began a seventeen million dollar project to replace sewers. The next year, the city dedicated a new incinerator, which processes not only the Twin City's solid waste, but that of surrounding communities.

As a further major improvement, the Twin City modernized and expanded its hospital, exactly thirty years after St. Catherine's Hospital opened in 1928. The Inland Steel-Ryerson Foundation contributed a million and a half dollars to remodel the hospital and to add a new wing dedicated as a memorial to L. E. and P.D. Block, sons of Joseph, and two of Inland's primary founders. Later the project was enlarged at a total cost of $6,577,000, with other industries contributing. In 1973, St. Catherine's Hospital dedicated the Colonel Walter J. Riley Special Unit, containing beds for intensive care, coronary care, and post-operative care following heart surgery. (Colonel Riley died on June 1 of that year at the age of 97.) In 1978, the Hospital Authority of East Chicago authorized issuance of $11,250,000 in tax-free revenue bonds for another St. Catherine's Hospital expansion program, and expansion and modernization was still going on in the late 1980s.

Meanwhile, the Twin City's highway system was dramatically improved. In 1952, Governor Henry Schricker opened the new million and a half dollar intersection of the Chicago-Detroit Expressway, just south of East Chicago on Indianapolis Boulevard. In 1953, aerial surveys were flown for Indiana's East-West Toll Road, and in October, the Interstate Commerce Commission approved relocation of the South Shore railroad tracks from Chicago Avenue to a route along the Grand Calumet River in Roxana and the planned toll road; construction on the 200 million dollar, 156-mile superhighway began in 1954. Three years later, the state highway commission began to widen Chicago Avenue all the way across the Twin City, from Gary to Hammond, widening the street to forty-eight feet and four lanes for the five miles from Route 12 to Route 41. The following year, the $101 million Calumet Skyway, now called Chicago Skyway, opened, giving Twin City residents and businesses easy access to Chicago.

In 1960, ground was broken for an overpass over Route 20 to start the Cline Avenue Expressway, a heavily traveled artery that was still being added onto a quarter of a century later. Its initial benefit was to give Twin City workers a speedy route to the burgeoning bedroom communities south of the Grand Calumet River. In 1973, Congress appropriated sixty million dollars to extend the Cline Avenue Expressway 5.6 miles, from its terminus near Columbus Drive, over railroad tracks and industry to Calumet Avenue and the Indiana Toll Road in Hammond, the most expensive stretch of highway in Indiana history. Slightly more than a decade later, that extension was complete, directly linking the Twin City with the Indiana Toll Road in two directions, and connecting it with every major expressway at the foot of Lake Michigan. Commuter rail transportation also improved when, in 1977, the Indiana legislature approved a $3.6 million appropriation to recapitalize the South Shore railroad, with additional funding coming from Lake and three other counties, all such funding being added to a twenty million dollar federal grant.

The most sweeping program of renewal, however, was one planned and implemented by the Purdue/Calumet Development Foundation, a not-for-profit organization and a joint project of

Until the sixties, most residents of the Twin City paid scant attention to their community's history because many of them had lived through it. Faced with its seventy-fifth anniversary, however, a group of citizens formed the East Chicago Historical Society, whose founders' meeting was held May 26, 1968. Officers elected at the meeting are shown here. In the front row were Rose LeVan, historian; Melvin Specter, secretary; George Huish, president; and Ezelyn Johnston, board member. In the back row were Paul Zahara, treasurer; Dan Simon, board member; Hubert H. Hawkins, secretary of the Indiana Historical Society; and Willard Van Horne, Jr., vice president. Missing were Mrs. H.E. Zoeger, third vice president; William Riley, first vice president; and board members Colonel Walter J. Riley, Mayor John Nicosia, M.D.; Robert L. Smith; G. Galvan; W. M. Young; Hans Peterson; Margaret Jones; A. P. Davis; and John Fox. Photo from the East Chicago Historical Society

Mayor John Nicosia and his wife Helen, the daughter of former mayor Frank Migas, led a Diamond Jubilee parade that stretched all the way from East Chicago to Indiana Harbor, symbolically linking the unidentical twins. Photo from the East Chicago Historical Society

One of the daily parades of the Diamond Jubilee had an old-fashioned theme, and featured this old-fashioned girl. Several people who had been in East Chicago at its founding participated in the jubilee, including Edith (Wickey) Zoeger, a genuine old-fashioned girl who arrived in East Chicago in 1889, and would have been born in the village had her mother not had to deliver her enroute. Photo from the East Chicago Historical Society

Twin City industry, government, and Purdue University to improve living conditions. Twenty-one Twin City industries and businesses sponsored the foundation, which opened its offices in Indiana Harbor in 1955, and contributed more than a million dollars to support it. The program was a massive one that demolished the original lakeside community that the Lake Michigan Land Company had built just after the turn of the century. And then some. From the mid-fifties through the sixties, the foundation not only planned for the renewal of the Twin City, but wrote its housing, occupancy, and revised zoning code. It built a high-rise (Lakeview Apartments) to house people being relocated, underwrote the not-for-profit Housing Progress, Inc. so it could develop the 255 unit Cal-View project, supported a low-rent housing program, developed Prairie Park subdivision (80 acres, 230 lots) for middle-income families, acquired 100,000 square feet of downtown parking space, and also acquired acreage for neighborhood parks.

After several years of planning by the Purdue/Calumet Development Foundation, renewal became visible. In 1957, the $1.3 million, 86-unit Lakeview Apartments, first structure in the rehousing program, was dedicated, and the city council authorized a $1.6 million bond issue for municipal improvements tied to the urban renewal master plan. In 1960, the Urban Renewal Administration approved a $9.4 million grant and a $15.1 million loan for the 367-acre redevelopment program in Indiana Harbor. In 1961, the foundation took applications for eighty-four lots in the first unit of the Prairie Park subdivision, where all structures were to be single family dwellings. Prairie Park was cut out of land bought during the "Baldwin Boom of 1912" by the Philadelphia Land and Improvement Company and sold after World War I to Inland's Indiana Harbor Homes Company at the time it created Sunnyside. Most of that land had lain idle throughout the history of Indiana Harbor, even though people who worked in the Harbor were desperate for suitable real estate on which to build homes. Its development in the sixties helped staunch the outward flow of people that had become an almost overpowering current. Also in 1965, Inland Steel told of plans for a major research center in the same vicinity, and donated land for a new junior high school (which became the Joseph L. Block School), as well as land for a new main library.

In 1965, construction began on the first two buildings in the $3.6 million Cal-View Apartments project in Indiana Harbor. The next year, the Department of Housing and Urban Development (HUD) approved $3.9 million in federal loans to the East Chicago Housing Authority for 212 dwelling units. It also granted $593,754 to build three neighborhood centers. The community's share was $296,830. Inland Steel and Youngstown pledged jointly to match any amount contributed up to $112,500. The community, led by industries, gave almost $300,000. In 1967, ground was broken for four model homes, the first of 153 medium-priced dwellings, on land made available by the Inland Steel-Ryerson Foundation, near the new Inland research center. That same year, HUD approved construction of 570 public housing units in the Indiana Harbor renewal area at an estimated cost of seven million dollars.

Renewal projects of one kind or another continued throughout the sixties and well into the seventies. In 1968, the St. Luke African Methodist Episcopal Church broke ground for a 120-unit apartment project in Indiana Harbor. That same year, ground was broken at 136th and Pulaski for a low-rent, ten-story building with 108 apartments for the elderly. Another high-rise

on Railroad Avenue in East Chicago on the site of the pioneering Famous Manufacturing plant, became the Nicosia Senior Citizen's Building. In 1970, the federal government awarded a $13,362,987 loan grant for a 346-unit project of family dwellings on thirty-eight acres fronting on 151st Street. In 1971, Inland Steel announced a major rehabilitation of two hundred housing units in Sunnyside. In 1975, construction began on the eighty-three unit housing project of Gudalupe Homes Inc., south of the Joseph L. Block Junior High School. The land was made available by the Inland Steel-Ryerson Foundation. In 1976, the Lake County Council approved construction of a new, $1.25 million Superior Court building in Indiana Harbor, which was part of a rehabilitation of the Indiana Harbor business district. To compensate for the loss of St. Joseph College, which in 1974 accepted title to Amoco's research and development facilities in Robertsdale two miles north of East Chicago, the council in 1978 approved issuance of $1.8 million in tax-free economic development bonds to construct a shopping center on the former college site in downtown East Chicago. It was named Riley Plaza in honor of Colonel Walter J. Riley.

Not only did the town renew itself, so did much of industry, the "Fabulous Fifties" exceeding even the twenties in economic growth. These good times were stimulated by the bad times of the Korean Conflict, which further depleted the Twin City's already dry labor pool. As the mills returned to a war footing, production reached new highs and expansion continued apace. Indeed, the decade seemed like one long series of expansions, especially by the steel mills. In 1952, Youngstown charged three new open hearths, and Inland tapped the first heat from a new 250-ton open hearth, first of four that would boost annual capacity by 750,000 ingot tons to 4.5 million. In late 1953, with the economy again booming, Youngstown and Inland pushed expansion programs as steel supply lagged behind demand. Youngstown also began trial runs on its new cold rolled sheet mill, the last major addition in an expansion program. That same year, Inland and Youngstown mills set new production records to help the Chicago district produce 20,650,000 tons of steel and edge the Pittsburgh district out of first place as the nation's leading steel-producing area.

In 1955, Youngstown announced plans for new tinplate facilties between Riley Road and 129th Street. Inland Steel disclosed a heavy schedule of capital outlays, and said it would build a seventeen-story office building in Chicago's Loop. Meanwhile, Continental Foundry was busily building tank hulls as part of an armor program awarded to Chrysler Corporation, and Sinclair's new catalytic reformer and Standard Oil's orthoflow unit began operations. In 1957, Youngstown started operations of a new seamless pipe mill, and in 1958, Standard Oil began construction of the world's largest crude oil distillation unit on property within the East Chicago city limits, the site that once had been Berry Lake. At the same time, Inland began work on a steel revetment to enclose 231 acres in Lake Michigan to be filled for future expansion.

After a pause during a late-fifties recession, the Twin City's economy came roaring back with such expansion as to test one's imagination. After steel rebounded decisively in 1961 and idle furnaces returned to production, absolute expansion mania seized the Twin City, as the two largest local employers took turns announcing major expansion plans. Inland began the succession of good news by announcing in 1962 a long-range expansion program. Stage one would last three years, and its

Working women, some of whom began in the mills during World War II, joined the spirit of the Diamond Jublilee by showing up at work in the latest pioneer fashions. Contrasted here against Inland's fascinating industrialscape are, left to right, Jean Templeton, Leona Bokkew, Cheri Christianson, Mary Such, and Jane Quasey. Photo from the East Chicago Historical Society

Kornelije Stankovich, the chorus of St. George Serbian Orthodox Church, was one of dozens of groups that celebrated the Twin City's ethnic heritage at the Diamond Jubilee. The previous year, the group had traveled from Indiana Harbor to Montreal to sing at the World's Fair there. Shown here is the record album from the group's Expo '67 appearance. Photo from the East Chicago Historical Society

principal element would be an eighty-inch continuous hot strip mill. At the same time, Indiana Governor Matthew Welsh signed a permit allowing Inland to fill 780 acres in Lake Michigan. Not to be outdone by Inland, Youngstown, in 1963, announced a $250 million expansion program. Inland, in turn, that same year announced phase two of its expansion program, which included a basic oxygen furnace shop. Meanwhile, Youngstown broke ground for a data processing center on 129th Street near the number two tin mill. In 1964, Inland disclosed the third stage of its expansion program, whose major element was an additional continuous line for producing zinc-coated or galvanized sheets. As if this were not enough, Inland in 1965 revealed plans for a major research center in Indiana Harbor. Youngstown then disclosed future expansion plans for the next four years, and the state gave a permit to the company to fill a triangular area of forty-two acres in Lake Michigan.

By 1966, the good times were rolling giddily. The Indiana Employment Security Division reported only 1.5 percent of the labor force in the Twin City-Hammond-Gary area was jobless. That year, Youngstown unveiled its new eighty-inch cold reduced sheet mill, while an eighty-four inch hot strip mill and a new blast furnace were under construction. Indiana Governor Roger Branigin viewed the start of construction of Inland Steel's new research center. In 1967, Youngstown dedicated its number four blast furnace, largest on the North American continent. Not satisfied with the massive expansion it had already completed or planned, Inland in 1968 announced a capital program that would raise steelmaking capacity by one million tons. The next year, Youngstown opened a mile-long elevated roadway from about 129th Street and Dickey Place over five railroads, all the way to the lakefront.

Rust

But there was a new dragon at large in the land. Competitors in what had become a world market began to challenge the supremacy of American heavy industry, and rust began to eat away at the invincible heart of the most industrialized region in the world. There had been warnings as early as the prosperous fifties, when a few plants sold property, new pipelines reduced the canal's importance, and conglomerates bought old-line plants and turned them into "cash cows." This other side of the ebullient industrial growth was symbolized by an event that occurred in the middle of the sixties. In 1965, USS Lead Refinery in Calumet loaded a tractor-trailer with six hundred bars of silver bullion, and shipped it west. Not far outside of Chicago, hijackers hit the tractor-trailer. The six hundred bars of silver have not been recovered to this very day.

Amidst the greatest expansion of steel plants in Twin City history, other companies with well-depreciated plants disappeared, or were milked to death. Changes in societal priorities and a gradual internationalization of the marketplace began to burden other industries, some to the point of collapse. Meanwhile, the indulgences of the permissive national society of the sixties filtered into the traditional old country work-ethic fabric of the Twin City and temporarily weakened it. Apart from wages that lifted most blue collar workers in the Twin City into the middle of the middle class economically, and demands of technology that obsoleted many physical assets and required massive infusions of capital, the greatest weakeners of local industry were

The hardworking Farrar Choral Club, which sang its way from the Depression into the postwar era, also knew how to relax. Mrs. Victor Szurgot was "potted" as posie of the evening at the club's closing potluck party, May, 1967. Other members dressed as flowers are Betty Lou Swentzel, left, and Mrs. Eugene Pospychala. Mrs. Henry Czuba, who planned the party, came as a bee. Photo from the East Chicago Historical Society

laws that reflected new values. Of these, the most debilitating were laws mandating that industry—long-time beneficiaries of unfettered smokestacks—reduce their air and water pollution to the lowest practical level. For all the social good they intended and accomplished in the long run, these laws greatly burdened Twin City industry, which bore the punitive extra costs like a horse carries extra weight in a handicap race.

Twin City industry continued to divert money from productive assets to pollution control to an extent that placed it at a permanent competitive disadvantage in world markets. In 1976, Inland Steel agreed to install a ninety million dollar recycling and filtration system, and as the cost of pollution control mounted, Inland reported to stockholders in 1978 that it had spent almost two hundred million dollars for pollution abatement during the previous ten years. Moreover, the cost of operating these facilities approached twenty-five million dollars annually. Meanwhile steel imports reached a monthly record of 2,200,000 tons in February.

The industrial erosion that began in the sixties continued into the early seventies, even as expansion mania did. In 1973, USS Lead began an expansion program, Union Tank Car busily fabricated components for barges launched in the ship canal, and

Kappa Kappa Gamma, organized February 22, 1919 to promote charity, culture, and education, celebrated its fiftieth anniversary by honoring its past presidents, shown here. In the front row were Evalyn Giffin, 1941-1943; Louise Walker Jarabak, 1966-1968; Lillian Murray, 1933-1935; Agnes Jones Reed, 1923-1924; and Mary Lois Clark, 1944-1946. In the back row were Grayce Middleton, 1964-1966; Fortunetta Murray Conlee, 1962-1964; Alice Weirich, 1960-1962; Mary Lou Johnson, 1954-1956; Mary Jane Lloyd, 1956-1958; Betty Lewis Lilly, 1948-1950; Ruth Albott Natale, 1952-1954; and Elaine Nicholls, 1968-1969. Photo from the East Chicago Historical Society

Kingmaker John Krupa, Democratic county chairman for many years, is shown here, center, keeping track of election returns. Krupa also was the driving force behind the organization of both the new, postwar American Legion Post 369, which became the largest in the state, and the related Harold Taps baseball team, which won the Senior American Legion baseball championship after World War II. Later, Krupa also became state commander of the American Legion. Photo from the Pastrick Collection

Four Twin City political powers of the sixties were, left to right, Mayor John Nicosia, Isabelino Candelario, Jesse Gomez, and Jay Given. Photo from the East Chicago Historical Society

Linde built new air separation facilities. In 1974 Lykes-Youngstown Steel announced a two hundred million dollar expansion, including addition of an eighty-five-oven coke battery. That same year, Inland announced the largest capital expansion program in its history, and began operating its new number two two basic oxygen furnace shop. Driven by the energy crisis that had panicked the nation two years earlier, Combustion Engineering in 1975 announced plans for a six million dollar expansion at East Chicago to produce larger coal pulverizers for electric generating stations. Also that year, Blaw-Know (nee Continental, nee Hubbard) moved personnel into a new office building on Railroad Avenue, and the following year it agreed with Chrysler on production of fifty million dollars worth of Army tank components over twelve months. In 1978, Inland started up its new number eleven coke battery.

None of these positive developments, however, could totally compensate for the effects of brutal worldwide competition, the OPEC oil embargo that triggered an era of energy conservation, and a severe recession in the early seventies. Although there were a few ups during the seventies, much of the Twin City's industry slowly slid downhill. Despite this, Sales Managment magazine in 1975 ranked Lake County, whose industrial heart was the Twin City, fourteenth in manufacturing output among all American counties, at $5.7 billion.

Rebirth

Heroic conventional efforts to renew the Twin City having proved insufficient, and with the "Information Age" threatening to transform the Twin City into a municipal Ozymandius, community leaders concluded that the Twin City could never again be exactly what it had been. And that was not only a life-saving revelation, but a springboard into a second life, one filled with abundant promise.

Rebirth of the Twin City was based on an acknowledgment that smokestacks had lost out to computer chips, muscles to brains, blue collars, lunch buckets and hammermills to three-piece suits, attaché cases, and microcomputers, and the rhythm of changing shifts at the mills to a relentless pursuit of an ever-improving quality of life. Since traditional heavy industry had become an endangered species, adaptation to change became not so much a question of choice for the Twin City as of survival. It would not do for the model industrial community to become the quintessential buggy whip in a time when there were no horses or buggies.

During the 1980s, and in a variety of ways, the Twin City moved into, and became a leader in, the Information Age. As it turned out, heavy industry was not dead, only changed. Since high technology comprises not only makers but users, the Twin City became a major user. Thus, steel mills in the Twin City committed themselves to computers and automation, and the unions seemed to understand the importance of doing so. While the gross output of Twin City mills may never be what it once was, it should be better, less being more. Instead of being the slayer of industry in the Twin City, high tech proved to be its savior.

In 1980, Inland dedicated a new computerized blast furnace, and in 1985, LTV and Sumitomo Metal Industries formed a partnership to produce coated electronically-galvanized flat-rolled steel for the U.S. auto industry. Also in 1985, Inland commis-

sioned its new two hundred million dollar continuous casting complex with the startup of a new slab caster. By 1987, Twin City steel mills could point to a number of solid accomplishments. Costs had been cut, productivity improved, and quality raised to its highest level ever. Both Inland and LTV operated state-of-the-art continuous casters to meet worldwide competition, and Inland was working cooperatively with Nippon Steel of Japan.

Beyond traditional industry, the Twin City became well equipped to provide if not unique at least excellent services. The the most apparent of these is health care. St. Catherine's modernized hospital is one of the most important healing places in the state, and as a major employer in the community an important economic wellspring. St. Catherine's, with all of its facets, along with the Tri-City Mental Health Center and the Tradewinds Rehabilitation Center, helped make the Twin City a focus of health care in the southern Lake Michigan area, and a major force in the health care industry.

As metropolitan Chicago penetrates deeper into the Information Age, it requires ever more people trained in the skills required of the age. Many of those people are coming from the Twin City, which positioned itself to train not only its own citizens, but others. Its huge De La Garza Vocational Center has already geared up to train hundreds of students in Information Age technology and related skills. And the community's new central high school has been designed around computers to enable students to learn better and faster, and to adapt to the new age. Complementing these, an increasingly computerized and comprehensive library system with specialized collections serves a number of specialized constituencies. Thus, like steel is and oil was, training and education in the Twin City have become a major industry.

Moreover, the ancient advantage that has blessed the Twin City since the glaciers receded has produced an important industry: recreation. Lake Michigan, as in the early days of Indiana Harbor, has once again become an aquatic recreation center second to none in northern Indiana. Slips in a new marina were practically sold out before phase one of the marina was completed. Hard by the most unbreachable breakwater in the Great Lakes, the two mile promontory that is Inland Steel's Plant Two, the marina is designed to grow and become better with time. As it is doing so, related businesses are or will be springing up and multiplying, businesses like boat manufacturing, commercial fishing, restaurants, shops, and others.

All of these new shoots of growth are nurtured by the spirit of the Twin City, which transcends municipal borders. It derives from a tradition of striving that anyone who has ever been associated with the Twin City understands. The Twin City is and always has been a port of entry for people, not only entry to the United States but entry to the American economic and social system. Through many generations, people have been able to make a start in the Twin City, and from that start work their way upward. That striving has produced a special breed of people, most of whom have become contributing citizens with an undefeatable will.

No matter where they live, those many thousands of people who have experienced the crucible of the Twin City remain emotionally tied to it and spiritually undergird it. And, as the Twin City enters its second century and its second life, that spirit will enable the new Twin City to succeed and to prevail.

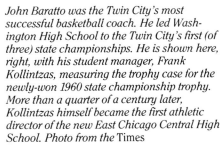

John Baratto was the Twin City's most successful basketball coach. He led Washington High School to the Twin City's first (of three) state championships. He is shown here, right, with his student manager, Frank Kollintzas, measuring the trophy case for the newly-won 1960 state championship trophy. More than a quarter of a century later, Kollintzas himself became the first athletic director of the new East Chicago Central High School. Photo from the Times

After owning Katherine House through almost a half-century of service, but with priorities in Indiana Harbor changing, the national Baptists sold the neighborhood house for a nominal sum to local citizens incorporated as Katherine House, Inc. Shown here is the signing of the legal documents for the sale. Seated: William B. Baker, president of the Katherine House board of directors in 1968 and Jesse W. McAtee, chairman of the legal committee. Standing, left to right were Louis G. Brannin, immediate past president of the board (1966-1967), Lowell R. Robertson, executive director, and Austin L. Boyle, president in 1963-1964. Photo from the East Chicago Historical Society

175

In 1964 the Twin City finally paid off bonds for the city water plant it had purchased in 1924, and immediately built a new one to supply water needs far heavier than the old plant could supply. Shortly thereafter, it opened a new water department building on Chicago Avenue. Shown here at the ribbon cutting ceremony for the new building were, left to right, Thomas Morris, W. Henry Walker, unknown, unknown, Al Vinick, Vince Kirrin, Mayor Nicosia, unknown, Mrs. Nicosia, and Father Campagna. Photo from the East Chicago Water Department

During the heyday of rock and roll, music teacher Nick Young (nee Ungarian) reintroduced the big band sound to Twin City audiences. To the surprise of many, the dance band he created at Washington High School became an instant hit and an institution, and membership in it became a matter of considerable prestige. The band's concerts not only drew large, appreciative audiences, but helped subsidize other music activities. Young himself moonlighted for years in the Kenny Knowlan Band, which played at Chicago's Embassy Club. He is shown here fronting the Washington Dance Band. Photo from the Young Collection

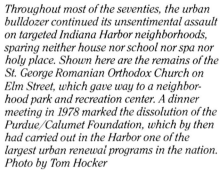

Throughout most of the seventies, the urban bulldozer continued its unsentimental assault on targeted Indiana Harbor neighborhoods, sparing neither house nor school nor spa nor holy place. Shown here are the remains of the St. George Romanian Orthodox Church on Elm Street, which gave way to a neighborhood park and recreation center. A dinner meeting in 1978 marked the dissolution of the Purdue/Calumet Foundation, which by then had carried out in the Harbor one of the largest urban renewal programs in the nation. Photo by Tom Hocker

Among the most familiar landmarks that disappeared from the Twin City landscape were these huge elevators of the Washington Lumber and Coal Company, which was established in 1912. The houses in the foreground are part of the western edge of the Park Addition to Indiana Harbor. The tracks in the background are the yards of subsidiaries of what once was the New York Central. Until bridged by a viaduct in 1929, the yards cut off communication between East Chicago and Indiana Harbor. Photo by Tom Hocker

1970s

The latest in men's seventies hair styles was modeled here by this worker at Linde Air Products Company. When Linde located in the Twin City in 1910, it produced less than one ton of compressed oxygen a day; forty years later it produced more than one thousand tons daily, and other products as well. Photo by Tom Hocker

As Latinos became the dominant ethnic group in the Twin City, demand increased for ingredients for food native to Mexico and Puerto Rico. During the seventies, Mexican food also became universally popular, further adding to demand for products distributed in the Twin City. Here a worker at Garza Wholesalers inspects dried chili peppers. Photo by Tom Hocker

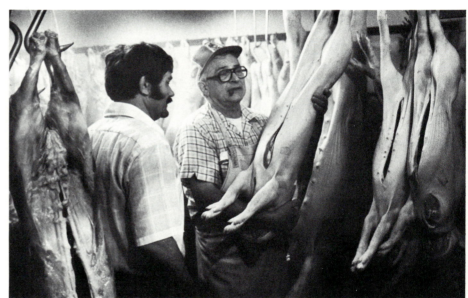

While it became voguish throughout the nation to preserve ethnic identity, Twin City residents continued to do what they had always done—assimilate very slowly. Here Dragomir Acamovich, in the custom of many Twin City residents, personally selects the meat that will be prepared and served to his guests in the style of the old world. Photo by Tom Hocker

In 1973, St. Catherine's Hospital dedicated the Colonel Walter J. Riley Special Unit, containing beds for intensive care, coronary care, and post-operative care following heart surgery. Shown here in front of the Colonel's portrait, which hangs in the hospital he founded in the twenties, are Colonel Riley's neice and two nephews. From left to right were Walter J. Riley II, Catherine Riley Leyden, and William J. Riley. Photo from the East Chicago Historical Society

While baseball, basketball, and football are major sports in the Twin City, the king of sports is politics. Here Mayor Robert Pastrick and supporters whoop it up after hearing the latest count in a hotly-contested election. Photo from the East Chicago Historical Society

Dr. Theodore Mason, right, East Chicago library director, presides over a system that has become comprehensive, computerized, and tailored to the special needs of local residents, educational institutions, and industry. He led the drive to add to the system a special facility to house a unique and growing collection of Twin City and Indiana historical documents. He is shown here escorting Massachusetts Senator Ted Kennedy during a visit to the Twin City. Photo by Mark Allan

The first Latino appointed to a major city office attracted this large crowd to his swearing in. Photo by Tom Hocker

In the ten years from the mid-sixties to the mid-seventies, the Twin City virtually replaced its basic services with new facilities and equipment. It replaced its water plant with a new one, built a new incinerator that services several cities, and dug up and replaced sewers throughout the municipality. Here a crew from the sanitary district begins work on the sewers in Sunnyside. Photo from the East Chicago Historical Society

When Inland Steel celebrated the start of its billion dollar expansion in 1975, Indiana Governor Otis Bowen ceremonially unloaded the first hopper of concrete into the forms. Fred Jaicks, Inland president, is to the left of the governor. Photo from Inland Steel Company

A municipal flag began to appear in the many Twin City parades. Two quarters of the flag feature crosses that allude to early Jesuit explorers; the other two feature beehives with thirty bees per hive, representative of Twin city industry. A vertical blue bar through the center refers to the ship canal. The standard bearers shown here were members of the Junior Police Patrol. Photo by Tom Hocker

Twin City hopefuls honed their talents under the tutelege of Babe Lopez, center rear. As an activity for youth, boxing found sponsorship in the Boys Club under the initial mentorship of Red McGregor. Eventually Boys Club programs combined with those of Katherine House. Photo from the Stuart Thomson Studios

181

In 1970, Shuffle Callahan, one of the Twin City's most famous fighters, sponsored a smoker for Little Pal Primmich, center front, another local fighting great. Everyone at the affair, seen in this photo, except ex-middleweight champion Tony Zale of Gary, center rear in dark shirt, were highly-regarded fighters from the Twin City. Two of the most prominent were Red McGregor, third from left back row, and Mickey Patrick, sixth from right, back row. Photo from the Stuart Thomson Studios

A stocked lagoon in Tod Park drew the attention of this happy piscator in the annual Twin City fishing contest. Although he did not win the contest, he certainly had the winningest smile. Photo from the East Chicago Historical Society

As in the early days of East Chicago, the saloon continued into the seventies as a center of Twin City social life, which this photo demonstrates. The corn stalk, upper left, suggests that this was the scene of a costumed Halloween party, but one can never be certain in the Twin City. Photo from the Stuart Thomson Studios

A sign of the times occurred in 1974 when the Reverend Viola Moore became minister of the Congregational Church, the first woman member of the clergy in the Twin City's history. She is ecumenically flanked here by Father Pusateri of Immaculate Conception and Father Fusco of St. Patricks. Photo from the Stuart Thomson Studios

American Legion Post 369 became the largest post in the state of Indiana. A prominent part of all Twin City parades and public celebrations, the philanthropic post also became one of the major financial supporters of worthwhile community causes. Photo from the East Chicago Historical Society

The Bicentennial parade held in the Twin City in 1976 was unlike any held in the nation, a statement from the ultimate mixing bowl. While Freedom's bell rang throughout the parade route, this Greek float reminded spectators that democracy did not exactly begin in Philadelphia. Photo from the East Chicago Historical Society

As competition for customers in a worldwide marketplace reached the deadly stage, Inland in 1980 unveiled a computerized blast furnace. It was one of many applications of new technology that local industry used to combat competitive cost disadvantages—labor, anti-pollution equipment, foreign-government subsidies—with ingenuity and efficiency. Photo by Tom Hocker

While many industries cut back production in the late-seventies and eighties, the green-house of Washington Park increased production of flowers and plants to supply a park system that had grown to ninteen municipal parks. Part of a drive to improve the quality of life in the Twin City, this renewed commitment built on a philosphy that originated in the twenties under the persistent leadership of James Thomson. Photo by Tom Hocker

New generations of Twin City residents, unaware of the way behemothian local industry once dominated the marketplace with brawn, were being trained in the subtler skills of the Information Age, even while learning and reinforcing the finer expressions of their forefathers' cultures. Here, Father John of the St. George Serbian Orthodox Church, leads a choir of youngsters in song to a patron saint. Photo by Tom Hocker

Former residents of the Twin City who move to the suburbs usually retain their ties to the community through membership in civic, church, and ethnic organizations, and pass the traditions of those organizations onto their children. Here, accordianist Jerry Tarka plays at a post-Easter Dyngus celebration at St. Stanislaus Church, located in his parents' former neighborhood. Photo by Tom Hocker

Cooperation among nationalities and races is represented in this prize photo taken at the Our Lady of Guadalupe Fair. The first pastor to Mexicans in 1920, Father Octave Zavatta, was a member of an Italian congregation. He conducted Mass in a Block Avenue store front for both Italians and Mexicans. When Our Lady of Guadalupe came into existence in 1927, the Missionary Catechists attached to it did social work among the black residents of the neighborhood, many of whom became Catholic. When the church burned in 1939 and was rebuilt across the tracks, the blacks stayed, re-built the old church, renamed it St. Jude, but continued to support special fund-raising events of Our Lady of Guadalupe, such as the fair. Photo by Tom Hocker

Even after several generations of people who have been born in the United States, the Twin City stubbornly holds onto its ethnic traditions and continues to be the focal point for many ethnic celebrations, such as the one shown here. Photo by Tom Hocker

Throughout the history of the Twin City, churches have been at the center of discrete cultural systems. In most cases, women members of the churches have been among the staunchest upholders of the cultural traditions of the church and of the church's constituency. Photo by Tom Hocker

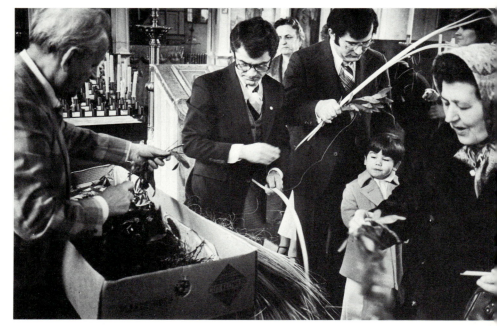

Twin City residents adhere to many customs that have endured the centuries, such as this Palm Sunday tradition practiced by members of the Holy Trinity congregation. The parish was organized in 1916 to serve one of the Croatian communities within the Twin City. Photo by Tom Hocker

Food has long been one of the most important sensual expressions of individual cultures in the Twin City, and nowhere has food been expressed in a greater variety of ways than in the bakery, a retail establishment that continued to be important in the Twin City long after the advent of the supermarket. Over time, bakers such as the one shown here, have become proficient in making not only American favorites, but in creating the specialties of more than one ethnic group. Photo by Tom Hocker

Toward recapturing its lakefront and establishing a new kind of industry, the Twin City broke ground for an extensive marina whose first phase was completed in 1987. Photo from the J.L.J. Miller Collection

What began as a cadre of a few Mexican strikebreakers in 1919 grew to become the preponderant ethnic element in the Twin City population mix. The knowledge of Latino influence in matters of community affairs is communicated by this confident woman on a Mexican Independence Day float. Photo by Tom Hocker

Twin City yachtsmen such as Herb Rimes, former owner of the Ford agency in Indiana Harbor, shown here, once had to travel to points as distant as Florida to engage in their favorite past time. With the new marina, people in the immediate vicinity of the Twin City are now able to find suitable water and facilities at home throughout the sailing season. Photo from the Stuart Thomson Studios

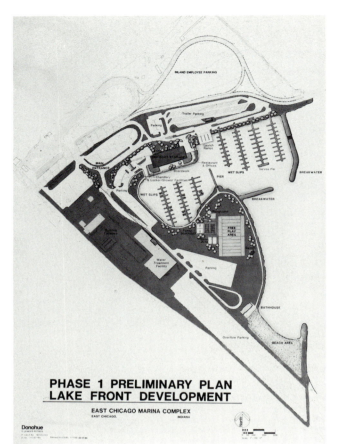

PHASE 1 PRELIMINARY PLAN LAKE FRONT DEVELOPMENT

EAST CHICAGO MARINA COMPLEX
EAST CHICAGO, INDIANA

Donohue

Phase one of the East Chicago Marina Complex provides more than 220 wet slips and an equal number of dry boat storage spaces, as well as launch ramps. Space was also reserved for locker rooms and showers, marine supply stores, restaurants, and administrative offices. At the same time, the beach, bathhouse, and recreational facilities of adjacent Jeorse Park were improved. The complex also anticipates a hotel/inn, additional stores and offices, condominiums, and expanded recreational facilities. Plan by Donohue Engineers and Architects

Viewed from Lake Michigan, the dry boat storage facility of the new Marina Complex looks like this. Drawing by Donohue Engineers and Architects

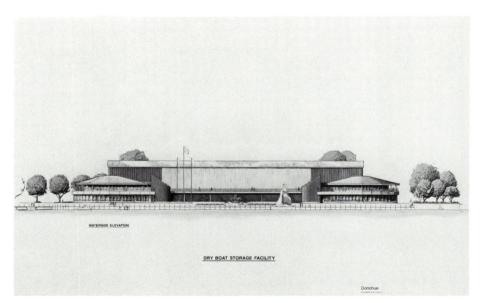

WATERSIDE ELEVATION

DRY BOAT STORAGE FACILITY

Donohue

As part of the rebirthing of the Twin City, two high schools built, in the main, shortly after World War I have been closed and an all-new school called East Chicago Central built. In this aerial photo it is shown while still under construction. Photo by Armando Gomez

Opened for the 1986-1987 school year, East Chicago Central was based on the latest technology. It was designed for the future and geared to turning out an improved version of the Twin City's most important product: well-prepared young people. Photo from the East Chicago School System

After a painful shakeout period during which obsolete industrial plants expired, viable plants re-tooled and re-programed, and new industry began to replace old, the Twin City entered a new era of optimism. This upbeat mood of the community is expressed here by Mayor Pastrick and his wife, Ruth Ann, in an informal talk to community leaders. As the community entered its second century, everything in the Twin City turned thumbs-up. Photo by Tom Hocker

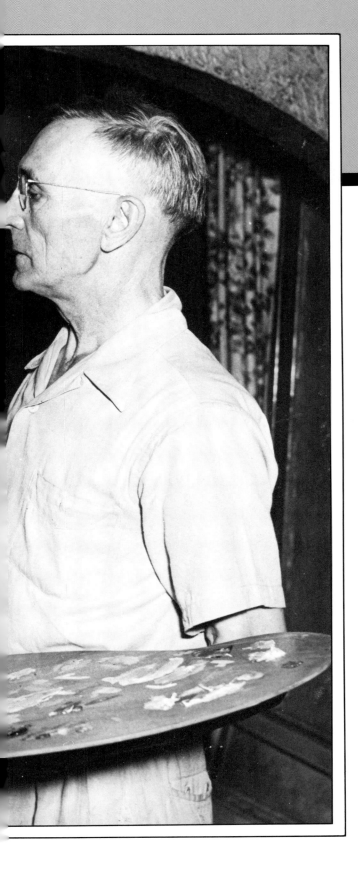

6

UP FROM THE CRUCIBLE

John Cowan Templeton, an itinerant sign painter who arrived in Indiana Harbor in 1908, became the world's foremost painter of the Indiana Dunes. And he did it the hard way. After working nights in an Inland Steel rolling mill, he would drive for the dunes to catch the morning light etching shadows in the yellow sand. After making oil-on-canvas sketches, he returned to his home in Indiana Harbor, where he did full-scale paintings, usually in his back yard. As no other artist, Templeton caught on canvas in brilliant colors all the beauty and savagery of the dunes. No one has ever painted them more vividly. Photo from the Jean Templeton Collection

The Twin City is a crucible, a melting pot, a container that resists great heat. For those who spend their formative years in the industrial colossus that is the Twin City, the experience is inescapably a severe test, a hard trial. But just as crucible steel is high-grade metal, the people who go through the crucible of East Chicago, Indiana usually emerge as high-grade people who add strength to their communities, wherever they may be.

Some of these people gain national prominence. In medicine, Hal "Sonny" Method, an All-American lineman and a surgeon, became chief of staff at Chicago's Northwestern Memorial Hospital, as did Dr. Sandra Olson. James Comer, a renowned child psychiatrist, became associate dean of Yale University Medical School. Nasif Mahmud became a distinguished expert on international law, and W. Henry Walker became a much-honored litigator known as the "Black Darrow." In religion, Warren Wiersbe popularized the gospel around the world, and Monsignor Michael Campagna created Hoosier Boys Town, a model for similar communities in other countries. In social work, Russell Ballard became the first male head of Hull House, the workplace of Jane Addams.

In the service of their country, Howard C. Petersen became assistant secretary of war, and his cousin, Richard Williams, became director of the Office of Chinese Affairs in the State Department. Nick Stepanovich became a shaper of national policy, especially on the relocation of displaced persons. Vince Mroz became deputy head of the Secret Service and once saved President Truman's life in a shootout at Blair House with would-be assassins. In the military, the Twin City has produced at least seven generals, and military heroes like Alex Vraciu, who once was the Navy's leading ace in the South Pacific, and Emilio De La Garza, Jr., a marine who won the Congressional Medal of Honor for heroism in Vietnam.

In sports, Coach Frank Thomas once built the best post-season bowl record of them all at the University of Alabama. Ray Weitecha became a perenniel All-Pro for the New York Giants. Vince Boryla became an All-American basketball player, an All-Pro, and an NBA coach, franchise owner, and operator. Harry Taylor became a fine first baseman for the old Washington Senators. Jim Platis became the holder of many records in amateur baseball. Pat Patterson played both professional baseball and basketball, with the Kansas City Monarchs and the New York Renaissance.

In the arts, singer Vivian Della Chiesa performed all over the world, in opera houses, on network radio and television, and in a variety of other media. John Templeton became the world's foremost painter of the Indiana Dunes. Wendell Campbell created many masterful pieces of architecture that helped build up Africa and the Middle East, as well as add beauty and function to many American buildings. John Leslie Edgeley wrote several novels and many radio scripts, and Steve Tesich wrote plays, novels, and screenplays, one of which, Breaking Away, won an Academy Award. Frank Reynolds wrote and delivered network news, and won an Emmy and a Peabody, as did a program that Archibald McKinlay nurtured into existence.

In entertainment, Marian Collier performed in hundreds of television programs and movies, and her brother, John Chulay, directed even more. Betsy Palmer starred in movies and in the long-running television series "I've Got A Secret." Jack Hubbard was a leading man in many movies and also starred in a television series. Mark Longorio became a rodeo champion. Stevie Wonder, who was born and spent his early years in the Twin City, became one of the most popular entertainers in the world, and the parents of Michael Jackson and the Jacksons are from the Twin City.

The Twin City experience, that testing time in the crucible, hardens those who go through it in a highly positive way. It prepares them for life, and sharpens their appetite for it. Those who grow up in the Twin City learn to approach life as a hungry person would approach a banquet table, and to feast on life for all of their lives. That finally is the story of the Twin City.

Monsignor Michael A. Campagna, an Italian immigrant, not only built (with his parishioners) Immaculate Conception Church with paving bricks discarded from Forsyth Avenue, he also founded Hoosier Boys Town in Schererville. A fifty-acre campus for wayward boys who are the innocent victims of misguided parents, Hoosier Boys Town has served as a model for similar projects in various parts of the world. Photo from the Times

Colonel Robert P. Lamont, president of American Steel Foundries from 1912 to 1929, served as secretary of commerce in President Herbert Hoover's cabinet from 1929 to 1932. Prior to his appointment to Hoover's cabinet, Lamont gained high visibility as a director in the Association Against the Prohibition Amendment. In 1932, he became president of the American Iron and Steel Institute, but after indicating a lack of sympathy with the NRA (National Recovery Administration), when three government officials attended an institute board meeting, he resigned in 1933. He called it "the beginning of government regulation of business," and added that "no one knows how far it may go." Photo from the East Chicago Chamber of Commerce

Jack Hubbard, son of an Inland Steel executive and named for the organizer of Hubbard Steel, became a successful stage and screen star for many years. Prior to service in the European theater in World War II, he was a leading man, and after the war he usually played second leads, frequently in westerns. In the 1960s, he starred in a television series loosely based on Culver Military Academy. Probably his most famous role was Turnabout, with Carole Landis. He once worked as an usher at the Indiana Theater. Photos from the East Chicago Historical Society

Vince Boryla excelled at more levels of basketball than any other mortal. He was the best basketball player ever produced at East Chicago Washington, an All-American at both Notre Dame and Denver University, an Olympic gold medal winner in England, an NBA All-Star, the coach and general manager of the New York Knickerbockers, a co-owner of the Utah Stars of the American Baseketball Association, and, as president of the Denver Nuggets, he was named NBA executive of the year. Photo from the East Chicago Hall of Fame Collection

General Ralph J. Canine, right front, served in Europe as a lieutenant in World War I and a General in World War II. During the latter, he was chief of staff of the XII Corps, serving from Normandy through the Battle of the Bulge, to the capture of Linz, Austria, and finally to contact with the Russians. In the process, he won the Distinguished Service Medal, Silver Star, Legion of Merit, Bronze Star with two Oak Leaf Clusters, French Legion of Honor, French Croix de Guerre with Palm, Russian Medal for Valor, Order of Defense of the Fatherland, and Luxembourg-Commander Ducal Order Courrene de Chene. He later became commander of the First Infantry Division. He is shown here in 1912 as a member of the Lotus staff, East Chicago High School's yearbook. Another celebrated member of the staff was Peck Gardner, left front, who became co-owner of the Big House in Indiana Harbor, Chicagoland's largest gambling casino from the late twenties to the early fifties. Photo from the East Chicago Historical Society

Howard Charles Petersen, son of East Chicago community leader Hans, in 1940 wrote the Selective Service Regulations (Draft Act) that affected millions of Americans during World War II. Afterward, he remained in Washington, first as undersecretary of war and ultimately as assistant secretary of war. He subsequently became chief executive officer for Fidelty Bank, Philadelphia, and a director of many boards and committees. Photo from the Clara Williams Collection

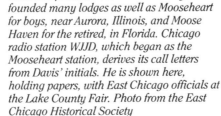

Dottie Vance turned her back on a career as a dancer and actress to become the first woman ever to go into record promotion, and she became one of the top three record promotion people in the world. She successfully promoted the records of such performers as Dinah Shore, Eddy Arnold, Perry Como, Roy Clark, Eddie Fisher, Barbara Mandrell, Donna Fargo, the Oak Ridge Boys, Lawerence Welk, and many others. She promoted for RCA, ABC, Dot Records, and MCA. She is shown here as a student at Washington High School in the early twenties. Photo from the Kathryn Schock Gale Collection and the East Chicago Historical Society

James J. Davis, secretary of labor under President Calvin Coolidge, reputedly worked for a time as a puddler at the Republic Iron and Steel Company in East Chicago. Like printers of the late ninteenth and early twentieth centuries, puddlers could take their trade with them from town to town, working for different employers. One of many steel people who traveled the well-worn trail from Wales to Sharon, Pennsylvania, to the vicinity of Muncie to East Chicago, Davis was

an ardent promoter of the Moose Lodge. He founded many lodges as well as Mooseheart for boys, near Aurora, Illinois, and Moose Haven for the retired, in Florida. Chicago radio station WJJD, which began as the Mooseheart station, derives its call letters from Davis' initials. He is shown here, holding papers, with East Chicago officials at the Lake County Fair. Photo from the East Chicago Historical Society

Alex Vraciu was the Navy's leading World War II ace, until being returned to the States in mid-1944. Flying a Grumman F6F Hellcat throughout the war, he shot down nineteen Japanese planes, destroyed eighteen more on the ground, sank a transport, and probably shot down two additional aircraft. He ended the war as the fourth-ranking naval ace. He survived service on six carriers, two of which were torpedoed, two ditchings, and two parachute jumps, and became known as "Grumman's Best Customer." After being shot down over Luzon in the Philippines on December 14, 1944, he spent five weeks in the jungle in command of 180 guerrillas. After the war, he became a Navy test pilot for the then-new jet airplanes. Twelve years after the war, he won the high individual air-to-air competition, outshooting all Naval and Marine pilots. He received the Navy Cross, Distinguished Flying Cross with two gold stars, and the Air Medal with three gold stars. He is shown here at a Block Stadium ceremony in 1944 being welcomed by Indiana Governor Townsend. Photo from the East Chicago Chamber of Commerce

Emilio A. De La Garza, Jr., won the Congressional Medal of Honor as a ninteen-year-old Marine in Vietnam. He gave his life to save comrades, displaying what his citation describes as conspicuous gallantry and intrepidy in action at the risk of his life above and beyond the call of duty. His citation reads: "Returning from a night ambush mission with his squad, while searching for the enemy, they flushed out two of the enemy, one had a grenade and De La Garza yelled a warning to his fellow troops. He placed himself between the two and took the blast, thus saving their lives at the expense of his own." In his honor, a mammoth training facility was built on Columbus Drive and called the Emilio A. De La Garza, Jr. Vocational Center. Shown here at the dedication of the center are, left to right, Dr. Robert Krajewski, school superintendent; Joseph Babas, director of the Center; a bust of the fallen hero; Mrs. and Mr. Emilio De La Garza, Sr.; and Mayor Robert Pastrick. Photo from the East Chicago Hall of Fame Collection

Wilfrid Smith was a renowned athlete, coach, official, sports writer, and editor. He laid the solid foundation for organized sports in the Twin City, coaching high school football, basketball, and baseball in the early 1920s. A strapping athlete of six feet four inches and weighing sometimes as much as three hundred pounds, Smith was the first four-letter-in-one-year athlete at DePauw University. He later played tackle and end on the Pine Village team that claimed the national professional championship before the National Football League was organized, and on the 1925 NFL champion Chicago Cardinals. He also played what then passed for pro basketball and minor league baseball. After retiring as a player, he was an NFL official, and sports editor of the Chicago Tribune. When offered the position of Big Ten commissioner, he declined. Smith is shown here, in cap and sweatshirt, with a prominent Twin City athletic club of the early twenties known as the Blues, Photo from the East Chicago Historical Society

Jim Platis compiled an amazing record of baseball durability and productivity that reflected national publicity on the Twin City. Beginning with Kiwanis League participation in 1938, Platis played organized amateur baseball for five decades, and was still facing ninety-mile-an-hour fastballs in 1988 when he was past the age of sixty. During that time he won nine batting champion-ships, the last one at the age of fifty-five, three league most valuable player awards, and was named to the Indiana American Amateur Baseball Congress (AABC) All-State team twelve times, and the AABC All-American team twice. A centerfielder, he played on twenty-five league, twenty-five playoff, nineteen state, seven American Legion, and five world finalist teams. He holds every amateur record for games played, runs scored, hits, walks, stolen bases, and years played. As a manager, he won seven league, six state, and two regional championships, while compiling a record of 210 games won and only 19 lost. He was inducted into the Indiana Amateur Baseball Hall of Fame in 1962. Photo from the East Chicago Hall of Fame Collection

197

Andrew "Pat" Patterson was, according to many observers, the finest athlete ever produced in the Calumet Region. A four-sports star, he played for Washington High School in the late 1920s and early 1930s and then at Wiley College, Texas. A star in two professional sports, Paterson played baseball with Satchel Paige and the Kansas City Monarchs and with the Pittsburgh Crawfords. He also played basketball with the New York Renaissance, the main touring black team prior to the Harlem Globetrotters, and one that many regarded as the finest professional basketball team of its era. Afterward, Patterson coached at Jack Yates High School in Houston, where his teams won three state football championships, four state basketball championships, and two state baseball championships. Not only was he inducted into the Negro Baseball Shrine, the black counterpart to the Hall of Fame in Cooperstown, but in 1982 he became the first black inducted into the Texas Interscholastic High School Hall of Fame. So universal was his success and fame that Patterson's sports memorabilia (sliding pads, etc.) reside in the Smithsonian Insititution. Photo from the East Chicago Hall of Fame Collection

Colonel Walter J. Riley, East Chicago's first city judge, founded the Twin City's largest bank system, attracted much of the industry to the Twin City, and founded the Manufacturers Association, the Carmelite Home for Girls, and St. Catherine's Hospital. He also coordinated munitions production in the Calumet Region during World War I, brought the Twin City home first in the nation in Liberty Bond subscriptions during World War I, and generally was a larger-than-life personality who influenced Twin City development to a greater extent than anyone else. For his benefactions and public services to state and nation, Pope Pius XI in 1928 made Riley a lord of the Knights of Malta, an order dating from the Crusades. Riley was one of only twelve Americans to be so decorated until that time, two of whom were Cardinals. Colonel Riley died in 1973 at the age of ninety-seven. He is shown here as a commission real estate salesman in early Indiana Harbor about 1905. From left to right were Theodore Norlin, surveyor, August Schnell, Officer Mike Gorman, Riley, druggist Oscar Goerg; and Charlie Egbert. Photo from the East Chicago Historical Society

Vivian Della Chiesa, whose family ran a confectionary store in East Chicago, was selected by CBS in 1934 as the finest voice in the Midwest, and went on to star in opera, network radio, television, and supper clubs for almost half a century. In 1936 she debuted as Mimi in La Boheme for the Chicago City Opera, and went on to sing in opera houses all over the nation and world. On an Australian opera tour, she once sang a different program in every major city of the country. In the late 1930s she starred in an incredible three network radio shows a week, and during World War II she sang for the armed forces and traveled throughout America selling bonds. About that time, she began to mix her media, singing not only operas and radio, but in concerts and in musical theater. She also recorded with the great maestro Arturo Toscanini, of whom she was a favorite. In the mid-fifties she turned to supper clubs, singing at such tony haunts as the Empire Room of the Waldorf Astoria, the Latin Quarter, the Coconut Grove, and night clubs in Reno, Las Vegas, and around the country. In television she guested on shows such as "The Firestone Hour," Milton Berle's "Texaco Star Theater," and Steve Allen's "Tonight Show," and later co-hosted a talk show in Chicago that was the forerunner of "Good Morning America." Her own show in Cincinnati, "The Vivian Show," ran for several years in the 1960s before being replaced by "Donahue." She continued to sing through the 1970s before beginning to teach voice. Photo from the Della Chiesa Collection

Frank Reynolds, son of an Inland Steel supervisor, was a network television anchorman and correspondent for more than a decade and a half, and won the industry's top awards. He won the George Foster Peabody Award for his defense of the press against former Vice President Spiro Agnew, he anchored ABC's Emmy-winning coverage of President Nixon's visit to China, and in 1980 he won another Emmy for his reporting on ABC News' post-election special edition. He reported from all over the world, anchored special coverage of the Senate Watergate hearings, and became chief anchor of ABC's World News Tonight. He also was first to anchor the Iran Crisis, a nightly report of the hostage situation that evolved into a regular nightly ABC program. His blue-collar pride-in-workmanship ethic also won him a permanent place in journalism textbooks with his famous "let's get it straight" command. Following the attempted assassination of President Reagan, colleagues prematurely reported the death of Press Secretary James Brady, which resulted in an on-the-air Reynolds outburst heard around the broadcasting world: "Let's get it straight. Let's get it nailed down. Let's end the confusion so we can report this accurately!" Sketch by Andrew J. Biancardi

Henry Milton grew up to be a baseball player of extraordinary talent, a decade or so before he could cash in on it. After becoming a legendary hitter on Coach John McShane's perenniel conference champions, Milton took his speed, sharp eye, and rifle arm to the Kansas City Monarchs, for whom he starred for eight years. A superstar constrained from performing in the then-segrated major leagues, the value of a Henry Milton in today's baseball market could only be calculated in the millions of dollars. He is shown here as a boy during the World War I period. Photo from the Walker Collection

Archibald McKinlay, shown here with Walter Cronkite in 1965, nurtured into existence the highest-rated public affairs program in the history of television. Called "The National Drivers' Test," the program generated more mail than any program ever broadcast, and it won the coveted George Foster Peabody Award, broadcasting's highest honor. Among many other productions, McKinlay also wrote and produced "A Mission of Beauty," a multi-media show that ran for nine months as a complement to the Louis Comfort Tiffany exhibition, and which was described as the finest show of its kind ever made. An author of several books, McKinlay also filled key positions in Washington during the Nixon administration. Since 1981, he has popularized the history of the Calumet Region, and attempted to give residents and former residents of The Region a sense of their heritage. Photo from CBS News

Mildred Carlson Ahlgren of Indiana Harbor was named one of the six most successful women in America in 1953 by the Woman's Home Companion magazine. This selection stemmed from her campaign of twenty years' duration to encourage women to play an active a role in public affairs, and from the fact that she was president of the eleven million member General Federation of Women's Clubs. Over her career, Mrs. Ahlgren campaigned to sell bonds, encourage youth, preserve historical records, promote the arts, combat Communism, and foster child welfare, among other causes. A strong believer in states' rights, she opposed federal aid to education. At the time of her ascendancy to the head of the federation, she pledged her support to the United Nations, and to deepening Americans' understanding of its importance. An important member of Washington society, Mildred Carlson Ahlgren entertained kings, queens, and even dictators. Photo from the Associated Press

201

James P. Comer, M.D., shown here as a student at Washington High School, became a child psychiatrist and one of the nation's foremost experts on improving the academic performance of low-income, socially under-developed minority students. He is the Maurice Falk Professor of Child Psychiatry at the Yale Child Study Center, and associate dean of the Yale University School of Medicine. Comer has authored numerous articles on adolescence for both professional and popular publications, several books (Beyond Black and White, Black Child Care, which he co-authored) and a monthly column in Parents *magazine. As a pioneer in testing the idea that social skills relate to success in school, Comer developed a model for creating an atmosphere conducive to learning, a model that substitutes an incentive to learn for an attitude of despair. Eventually applied to a number of schools, the model also evolved into a one-year fellow-ship program at Yale for teachers and administrators who return to their schools as agents of change. In schools where it has been applied, students surge ahead of other students in grades generally, and in language arts and mathematics particularly. Photo from the Robinson Collection*

Jean Shepherd, shown here as a child with Randy, the brother he immortalized in fiction, lived his early years in East Chicago, before moving two miles south to Hessville. He became one of the nation's leading humorists, a modern Mark Twain, often basing his stories on life in the Calumet Region. He has written several books of fiction, telecasts, and screenplays. His books include The America of George Ade, In God We Trust: All Others Pay Cash, Wanda Hickey's Night of Golden Memories, The Ferrari in the Bedroom, *and* Fistful of Fig Newtons. *His feature motion picture,* A Christmas Story, *has become an American classic. Photo from the East Chicago Historical Society*

W. Henry Walker was named DePaul University Law Schools's outstanding alumnus in 1985. Through a long career in which he has tried cases halfway around the world, Walker has been the defender of the poor and the rejected, and came to be known as the "Black Darrow." He was the organizing force of the civil rights movement in the Twin City prior to the movement's gaining national attention in the sixties, and has been a frequent guest at the White House. He is shown here, center rear, with his wife Dorothy and Dean Elwin Griffin of the DePaul Law School. Seated is Willie Passmore. Walker's rags to riches story will be told in the autobiography, We Need A Colored Lawyer. Photo from DePaul University

Ray Wietecha compiled the most outstanding record of any football player produced in the Twin City. After playing on the great Roosevelt High School teams of the mid-forties and Northwestern University's 1949 Rose Bowl champions, he became an almost perenniel All-Pro center while playing for the New York Giants from 1953 to 1963. He was named first team All-Pro five times, played in four Pro Bowl games, played on the 1956 NFL champions and runner-up teams in 1958 and 1961, and played in "the greatest football game ever," the sudden death 1958 championship game against the John Unitas-led Baltimore Colts. Later he coached with the Green Bay Packers, Los Angeles Rams, New York Giants, and Arizona Wranglers (nee Blitz) of the United States Football League. Photo from the East Chicago Hall of Fame Collection

Willie Passmore , who personifies the never-give-up spirit of the Twin City, and who is the least handicapped person in the Twin City, was named "Handicapped Person of the Year" in 1969. He is shown here with his mother, Laura Passmore, and foster-father in the rose garden of the White House being congratulated by President Nixon. Passmore's citation reads: "Your outstanding record of service to your community and the fact that you overcame a very severe disability mark you as an inspiration to all handicapped citizens. Through your range of responsibilities, you have helped countless disabled individuals to win economic independence and positions as contributors to community life. . . . You prove every day that the handicapped can, and do, produce and that it is good business to hire the handicapped." Although Passmore lost both legs following an injury in a football game, he finished high school and gained college credits while working as a taxi dispatcher. Subsequently, he did substitute teaching and wrote a weekly column for a black newspaper, while also counseling dropouts, raising money for the needy, finding jobs for the unemployed, giving jail inmates lessons in self-respect, and teaching Sunday school. Active in practically every community improvement organization, from the library board to the Diamond Jubilee Pageant, Passmore still finds time to visit patients at St. Catherine's Hospital every Sunday morning, and prisoners at Michigan City state penitentiary every Sunday afternoon. In 1965, he became coordinator of the East Chicago Neighborhood Youth Corps. Photo from the East Chicago Historical Society

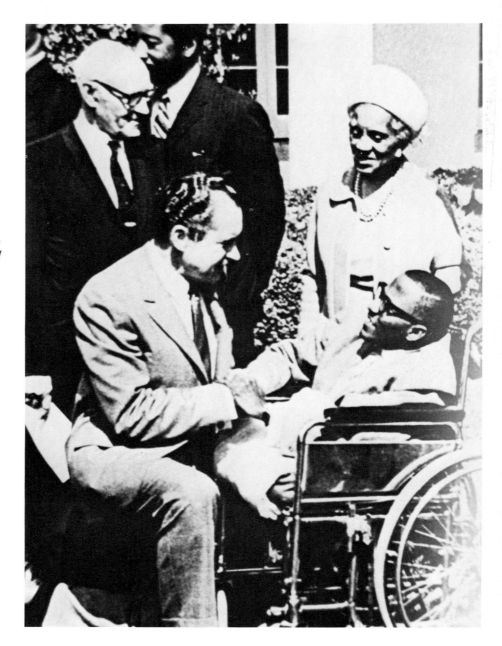

Betsy Palmer (nee Pat Hrunek) of East Chicago became a successful actress of stage, screen, and television, and is best known as a regular panelist of the television program, "I've Got A Secret." She vaulted to national prominence in "The Long Gray Line," one of the several movies she made, in which she co-starred with Tyrone Power and Maureen O'Hara. On the stage, she has appeared in such plays as Cactus Flower, (which she did on Broadway after Lauren Bacall left it), The King and I, Hello Dolly, The Prime of Miss Jean Brodie, and Ibsen's A Doll's House. In the fifties, she was a frequent guest of Dave Garroway on the "Today" show and with Jack Parr on the "Tonight Show," and also was hostess for a year and a half on the TV show "Girl Talk." More recently she has been guest star on such hit programs as "Murder She Wrote." Here she is shown with Mayor Robert Pastrick during a homecoming celebration. Photo by Armando Gomez

Steve (nee Stoyan) Tesich won an Academy Award for his screenplay Breaking Away, one of a number of screenplays he has written. He also wrote the movie, Four Friends, which was partially shot in East Chicago. He is shown here, left, on location. Tesich has also written seven plays, six of which were produced at the American Place Theater in New York. The best known of these is Baba Goya. Tesich also wrote the novel, Summer Crossing, which is set in East Chicago, where his family settled after World War II. Born during the war in Uzice, Serbia, near the border of Serbia and Montenegro, Tesich was separated from his family during the war. His father, a lieutenant in the Army under the Yugoslav monarch, went into exile after the German invasion and it was fourteen years before Tesich saw him again. His mother, whose family adhered to General Draja Michailovich, was jailed briefly and had to wait several years before being given permission to emigrate. At East Chicago Roosevelt, Tesich wrestled well enough to win an athletic scholarship to Indiana University, where he also anchored his fraternity's winning bicycle team in the Little 500, the race that inspired Breaking Away. Photo from the East Chicago Historical Society

Frank Thomas was one of the most successful college football coaches of his day. From 1931 through 1946, his University of Alabama teams won 108 games, lost only twenty, and tied seven, winning the Cotton Bowl, Orange Bowl, and Rose Bowl twice. His teams included such players as Don Hutson, the greatest pass receiver of all time both at Alabama and with the Green Bay Packers, and Bear Bryant, who ultimately became a legendary Alabama coach in his own right. As a player, Thomas led East Chicago High School to a win over Greenfield in 1915 for the Twin City's first state championship in any sport. At Notre Dame, he played quarterback for three years for Knute Rockne, barking out signals for the great George Gipp in 1920, and later playing with a quartet that became known as the "Four Horsemen." Of

Thomas' propensity for spending New Years in bowl games, Red Smith, the highly literate sports columnist, once said Thomas "was so much in California that he could have voted there." A Muncieite, Thomas is shown here, back row, left, in the backfield of the East Chicago High School team. Just behind and to the right of the center is John McShane, a three-sport coach at Washington High School who compiled an unprecedented record in baseball championships. Behind him, civilian wearing cap, is Floyd Murray, the first proper coach in the East Chicago schools, who later became a lawyer and was responsible for placing hundreds of Calumet Region athletes in college, including Thomas at Notre Dame. Photo from the East Chicago Historical Society

Nick Stepanovich, godfather of the Serbian community in Indiana Harbor, was the link between the United States and the Yugoslavian government in exile during World War II. A colonel in military intelligence, Stepanovich collected information among various factions in Cairo, and traveled to London, Arabia, Moscow, and elsewhere in a thrilling adventure that could have been a sequel to the movie Casablanca. His mission was to help the United States determime whom to support (Tito or Michailovich partisans) after the war. Having been born and raised in the Serbian enclave of Indiana Harbor, Stepanovich spoke fluent Serbo-Croatian and could communicate with all parties. After the war, Stepanovich traveled to camps throughout Germany and Italy, helping to formulate U.S. policy on the relocation of Yugoslavians, and arranging jobs for the dislocated and those dispossessed by the Communists. Many displaced persons (DPs) who came to the Twin City following World War II—the first significant influx of such immigrants in some thirty years—came under the auspices of Stepanovich. An avid anti-Communist, Stepanovich also supported a national uprising among those who remained loyal to the young King Peter, who himself visited Stepanovich in Indiana Harbor in 1948 and again in 1959. A confidante of many people in high places, Stepanovich was a guest in the White House of every President since Eisenhower. Photo by Thomas Hocker

Ed Rucinski, fourth from right in the back row, was an All-Pro end for the Chicago Cardinals. He started in the 1943 NFL All Star game against the champion Washington Redskins. Of that team, eight have been inducted into the Pro Football Hall of Fame. After starring at Roosevelt High School in football, basketball, and track from 1934 to 1936, Rucinski started at Indiana University for three years, started in the North-South bowl game in Montgomery, Alabama, started in the 1941 College All Star game against the Bears, and became the first draft pick of the Brooklyn Dodgers, a team coached by the legendary Jock Sutherland. He started for Brooklyn for two years before being traded to the Chicago Cardinals, where he challenged Don Hutson for the pass-catching title and played superlatively on defense, even while commuting to Chicago from Indianapolis to play on weekends. He is shown here as a member of East Chicago's Polish National Alliance basketball team, which included his brothers Al and Pete, the latter being the peerless coach of Roosevelt High School who for many years brought national attention to East Chicago. In the back row, from left to right were Mysliwy, unknown, Eddie Kumiega, Al Rucinski, unknown, Eddie Rucinski, and three unknowns. In the front were unknown, Stan Dubas, Hank Rogus, Pete Rucinski, and unknown. Photo from the East Chicago Hall of Fame Collection

Three members of the 1971 East Chicago Washington state championship basketball team played in the National Collegiate Athletic Association (NCAA) Final Four. From left to right were Junior Bridgeman, who played for Louisville, Tim Stoddard, who played for a champion North Carolina State team, and Pete Trgovich, who played for Johnny Wooden's UCLA national champions. Bridgeman went on to a twelve year career in the NBA, mainly with the Milwaukee Bucks, while Stoddard pitched for more than a decade in the major leagues. Photos from the East Chicago Hall of Fame Collection

Marian Collier (nee Chulay) became an actress who played in movies that were classics of the post-World War II era and television programs that practically chronicle the development of the medium. She is perhaps best known as Miss Scott, the female lead in the television series, "Mr. Novak." Among the more than a score of movies she appeared in were Some Like It Hot, *with Marilyn Monroe, Tony Curtis, and Jack Lemmon;* Breakfast at Tiffany's, *with Audrey Hepburn;* Bells are Ringing, *with Judy Holiday; and* Darby's Rangers, *with James Garner. Her television credits include: "George Burns and Gracie Allen," "Perry Mason," "David Niven Show," "77 Sunset Strip," "Peter Gunn," "Richard Diamond," "Zane Grey Theater," "Bob Cummings Show," "McHale's Navy," and "Marcus Welby," to name a few. She first came to public notice in 1953 as a member of the Don Arden Dancers in Las Vegas. Her brother John Chulay, once a star basketball player at Washington High School, is a Hollywood director who worked on the "Dick Van Dyke Show," "Mary Tyler Moore Show," and "Murder She Wrote." Photo from the East Chicago Hall of Fame Collection*

Frank C. Casillas, second from left, was born in Mexico and raised in Indiana Harbor. He became assistant secretary of labor for employment and training, having been nominated by President Reagan and confirmed by the Senate. He was the highest-ranking Latino in the labor department and one of the highest in all of federal government. He is shown here with Secretary of Labor Donovan and the Casillas family. Photo from the East Chicago Historical Society

California Is Popular With Foreign Travelers

California was the most popular U.S. travel destination for overseas visitors and Californians were the most active international travelers during 1983, according to the U.S. Travel and Tourism Administration's In-Flight Survey of International Air Travelers.

The report showed 32 percent of overseas travelers visited California during the year, followed by 30 percent for New York, 28 percent for Florida and 15 percent for Hawaii.

More than one-third of U.S. travelers to overseas countries were residents of California or New York. Nine percent were from Florida, followed by five percent from New Jersey and Texas.

More than half of all foreign travelers visited only one state, with 26 percent extending their trips to three or more states. Sixty-four percent of U.S. travelers visited only one country and 16 percent included three or more countries during their stay.

Total trip expenditures—excluding international air travel—were $989 per person for Americans traveling abroad and $1,143 for overseas visitors to the U.S.

Eighty-seven percent of the American travelers were repeat visitors. Seventy-seven percent of the foreign travelers had previously visited the United States.

VA Reduces Home Loan Interest Rate to 13½%

The Veterans Administration has reduced the maximum interest rate on VA home loans from 14 percent to 13½ percent effective August 13.

The one-half percent reduction marks the first drop in the rate since November 1, 1983, and will mean monthly savings of about $25 on an average VA loan of $61,000.

VA also took action to reduce by one-half percent rates on graduated payment mortgages to 13¼ percent and home improvement loans to 15 percent. Current loan rates on manufactured homes with lot and lot-only loans.

The change will not affect the interest rates of existing VA loans, which remain the same for the life of the agreement.

Frank Casillas Heads Job Training Agency

Frank C. Casillas, a management consultant and former corporate executive from Chicago, has been sworn in as assistant secretary of labor for employment and training by Secretary of Labor Raymond J. Donovan.

As head of the Employment and Training Administration, Casillas is the highest ranking Hispanic official in the Labor Department and one of the highest ranking Hispanics in the federal government. He was nominated to this position by President Ronald Reagan on March 12 and confirmed by the Senate

Casillas is one of 62 Hispanics nominated by President Reagan to full-time positions in the administration.

A native of Mexico, Casillas, 57, came to the United States when he was three years old. He is a graduate of Purdue University with a bachelor of science degree in engineering and later took graduate courses in mathematics at Purdue.

From June 1983 until his Senate confirmation, Casillas headed his own management consulting firm, Casillas Associates, in Chicago. He previously had been with Bunker Ramo Corporation since 1968.

Casillas succeeds Albert Angrisani, the Reagan Administration's first assistant secretary for employment and training.

Acid Rain Continuing Problem in New York

New data reported by the New York State Department of Environmental Conservation researchers reveals that acid rain contamination of lakes and streams extends beyond the Adirondacks to sensitive bodies of water in the Catskills and Rensselaer Highlands, DEC Commissioner Henry G. Williams said.

Governor Mario Cuomo recently signed the nation's first legislation aimed at combating acid rain. The new law requires utilities and industries in New York State to reduce emissions by 30 percent by 1991. Pointing out that 81 percent of the sulfur deposition in the Adirondacks and Catskills originates from sources outside New York, the Governor said he hoped the legislation would spur federal action nationwide reducing sulfur dioxide emissions by 10 million tons a year. To date, the Congress has failed to enact any comprehensive legislation on acid rain.

Secretary of Labor Raymond J. Donovan (far right) administered the oath of office to Frank C. Casillas (left). They are flanked by members of the Casillas family.

La Taunya Pollard, shown here with the 1977 Roosevelt state basketball champions, second from top on left, became the nation's best woman basketball player in 1983, winner of the Wade Trophy. She was chosen player of the year by the nation's coaches of women's teams. During her senior year at California State at Long Beach, she led the nation with a 30.5 points per game average, her single game scoring highs being forty-eight against Marist and forty-five against UCLA. In addition, she averaged nine rebounds and 5.1 assists per game. Because of an injury, she did not play in the 1984 Olympic Games. Pollard began her athletic career at East Chicago Roosevelt, where she led Roosevelt to two Indiana state championships. Photo from the East Chicago Historical Society

Max Goodman, a violist, was one of the first Twin City residents to gain national prominence for music. In 1927, he was selected as a member of the National High School Orchestra, the All-American team of music. The orchestra performed in Dallas for the annual meeting of the National Education Association. Goodman's selection was a tribute to the East Chicago Public Schools, which had several years earlier instituted systematic instrumental instruction as part of the regular curriculum. Indeed, Goodman was a member of the first elementary school orchestra, which was organized in 1919 at Riley School. When he entered junior high school, Goodman became a violinist in the junior orchestra, and the following year became a member of the senior high orchestra from which he emerged a solo violist. Photo from the East Chicago Chamber of Commerce

Richard Williams was one of the famous "Quiz Kids" of prime time network radio fame. As an adult, he became a foreign diplomat and eventually head of the nation's China desk in Washington—director, office of Chinese affairs, Department of State. A mathematical genius, Williams was known as "The Super Quiz Kid." During World War II, the Quiz Kids traveled the country selling war bonds; to view the show, people had to buy a war bond. They also made a motion picture short, and appeared on most of the popular network radio shows of the day, such as the Jack Benny, Fred Allen, Bob Hope, and Eddie Cantor shows, and, in turn, had top entertainers, such as Bing Crosby, as guests on the Quiz Kids' own top-rated show each Sunday at seven p.m. A natural diplomat, Williams started his State Department career in Hong Kong in 1958 and also has served in Tawain. He married his Chinese language teacher, and soon spoke Chinese not only fluently but without a dialect. When the United States and China opened full relations, Williams became the first U.S. consul in Canton. Photos from the Clara Williams Collection

Robert Elliot Tod, East Chicago's founder, later owned the world's largest yachts. During World War I, he became commander at Brest, France, America's vital port of entry to Europe. There he greatly improved the dock and the method by which critical war supplies were unloaded, and generally increased the military effectiveness of the port. When the port ran short of water and there was no money to build a waterworks, Tod spent two hundred thousand dollars of his own money to provide it. For these and other services, he was awarded the Distinguished Service Medal and the Navy Cross, was made first a chevalier and later a commander of the French Legion of Honor, and received the Order of the Crown of Italy and the New York State Conspicuous Service Medal. After the war, in 1921 he became commissioner of immigration at Ellis Island, where he eliminated certain abuses in the service. He also participated in the defense of the America's Cup, and in 1911, launched the Katrina, the largest private yacht afloat at the time. Photo from the Anne Johnston Collection

BIBLIOGRAPHY

Ball, Timothy H. *Encyclopedia of Genealogy and Biography of Lake County, Indiana, 1834-1904.* Chicago, New York: The Lewis Publishing Company, 1904.

Bolton, Floyd B., John P. Fox, James P. Petronella, and Lillian Sowerby, *East Chicago, A Historical Description.* East Chicago: East Chicago Public Schools, 1947.

Boyle, Austin, "East Chicago, 1945-1985." (Typewritten MS in possession of Cattails Press, Chicago.)

The Calumet News. 1923—

Canal, Indiana Harbor—East Chicago. Chicago: East Chicago Company, 1910.

Cannon, Thomas H., Loring, H. H., and Robb, Charles J. (eds.). *History of the Lake and Calumet Region of Indiana.* (2 vols.) Indianapolis: Historians' Association, 1927.

Diamond Jubilee Historical Record. East Chicago: City of East Chicago, 1968.

East Chicago, Indiana. East Chicago: East Chicago Chamber of Commerce, 1925-29.

East Chicago Gazette, September 14, 1895.

East Chicago—Indiana Harbor. Chicago: East Chicago Company, 1910.

East Chicago—Indiana Harbor, Indiana. East Chicago: City of East Chicago, 1913.

Howat, William F. (ed.), *A Standard History of Lake County, Indiana and the Calumet Region.* (2 vols.) Chicago: The Lewis Publishing Company, 1915.

Indiana Harbor, The New Industrial City. Chicago: East Chicago Company, 1904.

Lane, James B., Escobar, Edward J. (eds.), *Forging A Community, The Latino Experience in Northwest, Indiana, 1919-1975.* Chicago: Cattails Press, 1987.

Miller, Simon *Ethnic Minorities In The East Chicago Community.* East Chicago: East Chicago Community Council, 1959.

McKinlay, Archibald *East Chicago: The Early Years.* Chicago: Calumet Roots, The McKinlay Historical Series Number Three, 1984.

McKinlay, Archibald *Swamp Baron.* Chicago: The McKinlay Communications Group, 1981.

Moore, Powell A. *The Calumet Region, Indiana's Last Frontier.* Indianapolis: Indiana Historical Bureau, 1959. Reprinted with an *Afterword* by Lance Trusty, 1977.

Perry W. A. *A History of Inland Steel Company and the Indiana Harbor Works.* Chicago: Inland Steel Company, 1980.

Police Departments of East Chicago, Indiana Harbor and Whiting, Indiana. Chicago: Wilkinson-Ryan Company, Chicago, 1914.

The Times (Hammond; also titled the *Lake County Times* and the *Hammond Times*). 1906-1987.

Twin City Sentinel. July 4, 1905.

Numerous documents and audiotapes of the East Chicago Historical Society. (Indiana Room, East Chicago Main Library.)

Numerous audiotape interviews conducted by the author.

INDEX